First World War
and Army of Occupation
War Diary
France, Belgium and Germany

24 DIVISION
Divisional Troops
Royal Army Medical Corps
74 Field Ambulance
1 June 1915 - 31 May 1919

WO95/2202/3

The Naval & Military Press Ltd
www.nmarchive.com
Published in association with The National Archives

Published by

The Naval & Military Press Ltd

Unit 10 Ridgewood Industrial Park,

Uckfield, East Sussex,

TN22 5QE England

Tel: +44 (0) 1825 749494

www.naval-military-press.com

www.nmarchive.com

This diary has been reprinted in facsimile from the original. Any imperfections are inevitably reproduced and the quality may fall short of modern type and cartographic standards.

© Crown Copyright
Images reproduced by permission of The National Archives, London, England, 2015.

Contents

Document type	Place/Title	Date From	Date To
Heading	WO95/2202/3 74 Field Ambulance		
Heading	74th Fld Ambulance Aug 1915 May 1919		
Heading	24th Division 74th F.A. Amb Aug to Oct 15 Dec 18		
War Diary	Eastbourme	21/08/1915	23/08/1915
War Diary	Bullswater	24/08/1915	01/09/1915
War Diary	Bullswater Southampton	01/09/1915	01/09/1915
War Diary	Havre	02/09/1915	03/09/1915
War Diary	Maresquel	04/09/1915	04/09/1915
War Diary	Neuville Sous Montr	05/09/1915	05/09/1915
War Diary	Neuville	06/09/1915	06/09/1915
War Diary	Lebiez	07/09/1915	19/09/1915
War Diary	Neuville S. Montreuil	20/09/1915	20/09/1915
War Diary	Neuville	21/09/1915	21/09/1915
War Diary	Radinghem	22/09/1915	22/09/1915
War Diary	Berguette	23/09/1915	23/09/1915
War Diary	Le Cornet	24/09/1915	24/09/1915
War Diary	Bethune	25/09/1915	25/09/1915
War Diary	Beauvry	26/09/1915	27/09/1915
War Diary	Beuvry	28/09/1915	28/09/1915
War Diary	Annezin	29/09/1915	29/09/1915
War Diary	Bourecq	30/09/1915	30/09/1915
Heading	No. 74. 7. a		
War Diary	Bourecq	01/10/1915	01/10/1915
War Diary	Proven	02/10/1915	05/10/1915
War Diary	Hillehoek	06/10/1915	10/10/1915
War Diary	Boeschepe	11/10/1915	31/10/1915
Heading	24th Division 74th F.A. Vol. 3 Nov 15		
War Diary	Boeschepe	01/11/1915	22/11/1915
War Diary	Eecke	23/11/1915	23/11/1915
War Diary	Oehtezeele	24/11/1915	24/11/1915
War Diary	Houlle	25/11/1915	25/11/1915
War Diary	Chateau De La Viergette (Eperleques)	26/11/1915	26/11/1915
War Diary	Chateau De La Viergette	27/11/1915	27/11/1915
War Diary	Ch. De La. V.	28/11/1915	30/11/1915
Heading	24th Div. 74th F.a. Vol. 3		
War Diary	Chateau De La Viergette (Eperleques)	01/12/1915	01/12/1915
War Diary	Ch. de La V.	02/12/1915	20/12/1915
War Diary	Ch De La Viergette	21/12/1915	21/12/1915
War Diary	Ch De La V.	22/12/1915	31/12/1915
Heading	24th Div Jan 1916 74th F.A. Vol 4		
War Diary	Ch. De La Viergette Westrove	01/01/1916	01/01/1916
War Diary	Ch De La V	02/01/1916	06/01/1916
War Diary	Poperinghe	07/01/1916	31/01/1916
Heading	Feb 1916 74th Field Ambulance		
Heading	74th F.A. Vol 5		
War Diary	Poperinghe	01/02/1916	29/02/1916
Heading	March 1916 74 F. Amb Vol 6		
War Diary	Poperinghe	01/03/1916	20/03/1916
War Diary	Bethune	21/03/1916	29/03/1916
War Diary	Bailleul	30/03/1916	31/03/1916

Heading	24th Div April 1916 No. 74 F. amb		
War Diary	Bailleul	01/04/1916	30/04/1916
Heading	24th Div May 1916 No. 74 F. amb		
War Diary	Bailleul	01/05/1916	31/05/1916
Heading	June 1916 No. 74 F.a.		
War Diary	Bailleul	01/06/1915	30/06/1916
Miscellaneous	Memorandum.	02/09/1916	02/09/1916
Heading	24th Division July 1916 74th Field Ambulance		
Miscellaneous	HQ. 24th Division		
War Diary	Mont Noir	01/07/1916	20/07/1916
War Diary	Meteren	22/07/1916	24/07/1916
War Diary	Cavillon (Somme)	25/07/1916	25/07/1916
War Diary	Cavillon	26/07/1916	31/07/1916
Heading	24th Div August 1916 74th Field Ambulance		
War Diary	Corbie (Somme)	01/08/1916	01/08/1916
War Diary	Corbie	02/08/1916	26/08/1916
War Diary	Buire Sur-L'Ancre.	27/08/1916	28/08/1916
War Diary	Buire	29/08/1916	29/08/1916
War Diary	Albert	30/08/1916	31/08/1916
Heading	24th Div Sept 1916 74th Field Ambulance		
War Diary	Albert	01/09/1916	04/09/1916
War Diary	Buire	05/09/1916	06/09/1916
War Diary	Ergnies	07/09/1916	19/09/1916
War Diary	Pressy	20/09/1916	22/09/1916
War Diary	Houdain	23/09/1916	24/09/1916
War Diary	Estree Cauchie	25/09/1916	25/09/1916
War Diary	Estree	26/09/1916	30/09/1916
Heading	24th Div Oct 1916 74th Field Ambulance		
War Diary	Estree Cauchy	01/10/1916	01/10/1916
War Diary	Estree	02/10/1916	25/10/1916
War Diary	Estree Cauchee	26/10/1916	27/10/1916
War Diary	Labeuvriere	28/10/1916	31/10/1916
War Diary	24th Div Nov 1916 74th Field Ambulance		
Miscellaneous	24 Division		
War Diary	Labeuvriere	01/11/1916	30/11/1916
Heading	24th Div Dec 1916 74th Field Ambulance		
War Diary	Labeuvriere	01/12/1916	31/12/1916
Heading	24th Div. Jan 1917 74th Field Ambulance		
War Diary	Labeuvriere	01/01/1917	31/01/1917
Heading	24th Div Feb 1917 74th Field Ambulance		
War Diary	Labeuvriere	01/02/1917	28/02/1917
Heading	24th Div. Mar 1917 74th Field Ambulance		
War Diary	Labeuvriere	01/03/1917	04/03/1917
War Diary	Fosse 10 Petit Sains	05/03/1917	05/03/1917
War Diary	Fosse 10	06/03/1917	31/03/1917
Heading	24th Div April 1917 74th F.A.		
War Diary	Fosse 10 Petit Sains	01/04/1917	01/04/1917
War Diary	Fosse 10	02/04/1917	19/04/1917
War Diary	Ecquedecques	20/04/1917	23/04/1917
War Diary	Lisbourg	24/04/1917	25/04/1917
War Diary	Ecquedecques	26/04/1917	26/04/1917
War Diary	Bethune	27/04/1917	03/05/1917
Miscellaneous	B.E.F. Summary Of Medical War Diaries Of 73rd Field Ambulance		
War Diary	Casualties	01/04/1917	01/04/1917
War Diary	Med. Arr	02/04/1917	02/04/1917

War Diary	Operation Enemy		
War Diary	Operation Enemy & Casualties	04/04/1917	05/04/1917
War Diary	Med. Arr	09/04/1917	09/04/1917
War Diary	Accident & Casualties	09/04/1917	10/04/1917
War Diary	Med. Arr	11/04/1917	11/04/1917
War Diary	Operation Casualties	12/04/1917	12/04/1917
War Diary	Operation Enemy	14/04/1917	14/04/1917
War Diary	Operation & Evacuation	15/04/1917	15/04/1917
War Diary	Evacuation	17/04/1917	17/04/1917
War Diary	Med. Arr.	19/04/1917	19/04/1917
War Diary	Moves	20/04/1917	20/04/1917
War Diary	Transfer	21/04/1917	21/04/1917
War Diary	Moves	24/04/1917	27/04/1917
War Diary	Appointment	30/04/1917	30/04/1917
War Diary	Casualties	01/04/1917	01/04/1917
War Diary	Med. Arr	02/04/1917	02/04/1917
War Diary	Operation Enemy	02/04/1917	02/04/1917
War Diary	Operation Enemy & Casualties	04/04/1917	05/04/1917
War Diary	Med. Arr	09/04/1917	09/04/1917
War Diary	Accident & Casualties	10/04/1917	10/04/1917
War Diary	Med. Arr	11/04/1917	11/04/1917
War Diary	Operation Casualties	12/04/1917	12/04/1917
War Diary	Operation Enemy	14/04/1917	14/04/1917
War Diary	Operation & Evacuation	15/04/1917	15/04/1917
War Diary	Evacuation	17/04/1917	17/04/1917
War Diary	Med. Arr	19/04/1917	19/04/1917
War Diary	Moves	20/04/1917	20/04/1917
War Diary	Transfer	21/04/1917	21/04/1917
War Diary	Moves	24/04/1917	27/04/1917
War Diary	Appointment	30/04/1917	30/04/1917
Heading	May 1917 No. 74 F.a.		
War Diary	Bethune	01/05/1917	06/05/1917
War Diary	Malanoy Farm	07/05/1917	09/05/1917
War Diary	Robecq	10/05/1917	10/05/1917
War Diary	Hazebrouck	11/05/1917	11/05/1917
War Diary	Steenvoorde	12/05/1917	14/05/1917
War Diary	Poperinghe	15/05/1917	25/05/1917
War Diary	In The Field 20 C 5 L H5 E T.28	26/05/1917	26/05/1917
War Diary	C. 20. C. 5.6	27/05/1917	28/05/1917
War Diary	G. 20. C. 5.6 Sheet 8	29/05/1917	31/05/1917
Miscellaneous	B.E.F. Summary Of Medical War Diaries Of 73rd Field Ambulance		
War Diary	Operation Enemy & Casualties	01/05/1917	04/05/1917
War Diary	Moves	05/05/1917	05/05/1917
War Diary	Moves & Transfer	10/05/1917	10/05/1917
War Diary	Operation Enemy & Casualties	01/05/1917	04/05/1917
War Diary	Moves	05/05/1917	05/05/1917
War Diary	Moves & Transfer	10/05/1917	10/05/1917
Heading	June 1917 No 74. F.a.		
Miscellaneous	D A.& Q.M.G 24th Division		
War Diary	H 15 C 3.1 Sheet 27	01/06/1917	03/06/1917
War Diary	G 20. C. 5.6 Sheet 28	04/06/1917	05/06/1917
War Diary	M 5 Achieve Sheet 28	06/06/1917	06/06/1917
War Diary	M 5. d Central Sheet 28	07/06/1917	29/06/1917
War Diary	Lumbres Sheet 5A Hazebrouck		
War Diary	Alincthun Sheet Calais	30/06/1917	30/06/1917

Heading	July 1917 74th F.A.		
War Diary	Alincthun Sheet Calais	01/07/1917	17/07/1917
War Diary	Lumbres Sheet 5A Hazebrouck	18/07/1917	18/07/1917
War Diary	Renescure	19/07/1917	19/07/1917
War Diary	Caestre	20/07/1917	20/07/1917
War Diary	Eecke	21/07/1917	21/07/1917
War Diary	Steenvoorde	22/07/1917	22/07/1917
War Diary	Reninghelst	22/07/1917	31/07/1917
Heading	Aug 1917 No 74 F.A.		
War Diary	Reninghelst. G. 34.b.20 Sheet 28	01/08/1917	16/08/1917
War Diary	Reninghelst	17/08/1917	31/08/1917
Heading	Sept 1917 No 74 F.A.		
Miscellaneous	74th F.A. R.A.M.C.		
War Diary	G. 34. b. 20. Sheet 28	01/09/1917	16/09/1917
War Diary	F. 2. d 4.8. Sheet 36A	16/09/1917	20/09/1917
War Diary	P. 25 Sheet 57c	22/09/1917	26/09/1917
War Diary	C. 23 Sheet 62c	27/09/1917	29/09/1917
War Diary	Sheet 62c Q 28 6.1.5	29/09/1917	30/09/1917
Heading	War Diary of 74th Field Ambulance for October 1917		
War Diary	Q. 28. d.8.9 Sheet 62c	01/10/1917	16/10/1917
War Diary	Q. 28.d.8.9	17/10/1917	31/10/1917
Heading	War Diary 74th Field Ambulance Nov 1st To Nov 30th 1917		
War Diary	Q. 28. d.8.9 Sheet 62c	01/11/1917	30/11/1917
Heading	Dec 1917 No 74 F. A.		
War Diary	Q. 28. d.8.9	01/12/1917	08/12/1917
War Diary	Bernes	09/12/1917	31/12/1917
Heading	Jan 1918 No 74. F.a.		
War Diary	Bernes	01/01/1918	27/01/1918
War Diary	Roisel K. 16.d.8. Sheet 25	28/01/1918	31/01/1918
Heading	Feb 1918 No. 74 F.a.		
War Diary	Sheet 62c K 16. d.8.1	01/02/1918	12/02/1918
War Diary	K. 16. d.8.1. Roisel	13/02/1918	22/02/1918
War Diary	Sheet 62c K 16 d 81	23/02/1918	28/02/1918
Heading	Mar 1918 74th Field Ambulance		
War Diary	Sheet 62c V 5d 37	01/03/1918	12/03/1918
War Diary	W 2 a 31 Sheet 62c	13/03/1918	13/03/1918
War Diary	Sheet 62c. W2 a31	14/03/1918	22/03/1918
War Diary	O 30c 53	23/03/1918	23/03/1918
War Diary	Chaulne		
War Diary	Hallu Sheet 62D	24/03/1918	24/03/1918
War Diary	Lihons Sheet 62D	25/03/1918	25/03/1918
War Diary	Cayeux Sheet 62E D. 6	26/03/1918	27/03/1918
War Diary	Rouvrel Sheet 66c H.3	28/03/1918	28/03/1918
War Diary	St. Sauflieu Sheet Amiens	29/03/1918	29/03/1918
War Diary	Sains-En Amiennois Sheet 66E A.2.a	30/03/1918	31/03/1918
Heading	War Diary For Month Of April		
War Diary	Sheet Amiens 17 Sains-En-Amiennois	01/04/1918	03/04/1918
War Diary	Boves	04/04/1918	06/04/1918
War Diary	Saleux	07/04/1918	07/04/1918
War Diary	Molliere	08/04/1918	17/04/1918
War Diary	Woincourt (Abbeville In)	18/04/1918	18/04/1918
War Diary	Orlencourt (Lens) Sheet 36B	19/04/1918	29/04/1918
War Diary	Orlencourt Sheet Lens.11A	30/04/1918	30/04/1918
Heading	May 1918 No. 74 F.a.		
War Diary	Orlencourt Sheet Lens	01/05/1918	01/05/1918

War Diary	Hermin (Lens II)	02/05/1918	02/05/1918
War Diary	Gd. Servins Sheet 36 B Q 36a. 2.5.	03/05/1918	11/05/1918
War Diary	Q 36 a. 2.5 Sheet 36B	12/05/1918	31/05/1918
Heading	June 1918 74th F.A.		
War Diary	Q 36.a. 25. Sheet 44B.	01/06/1918	24/06/1918
War Diary	Q 34.a 2.5	25/06/1918	30/06/1918
Heading	July 1918 No. 74 F.A.		
War Diary	Q. 34.a. 2.5. Sheet 44B	01/07/1918	31/07/1918
Heading	War Diary of 74th Field Ambulance from 1/8/1918 to 31st/8/1918		
War Diary	Q 34a. 25 Sheet 44B	01/08/1918	20/08/1918
War Diary	R. 8. c. Sheet 44B	21/08/1918	24/08/1918
War Diary	Sheet 44 B R 8 Central	25/08/1918	31/08/1918
Heading	Sept 1918 74th F. Amb.		
War Diary	R. 8 Central Sheet 44 B	01/09/1918	30/09/1918
Heading	Oct 1918 74th F. A		
War Diary	Ivergny 57C Sheet (N.20)	01/10/1918	06/10/1918
War Diary	Graincourt (Sheet 57c)	07/10/1918	07/10/1918
War Diary	Anneux	08/10/1918	08/10/1918
War Diary	Nieronies	09/10/1918	11/10/1918
War Diary	Avesags-Les Aubers	12/10/1918	16/10/1918
War Diary	Cagnoncles	17/10/1918	18/10/1918
War Diary	(B.4.a.98) Sheet 59 B	19/10/1918	19/10/1918
War Diary	Cambrai (Fan. St Druon)	21/10/1918	24/10/1918
War Diary	Cagnoncles B 4a 98 (57B)	25/10/1918	25/10/1918
War Diary	St Aubert U 18d 99 (51 A)	26/10/1918	31/10/1918
Heading	Nov 1918 74th F.A.		
War Diary	St Aubert U 18d 99 (51 A)	01/11/1918	01/11/1918
War Diary	St Aubert V. 13 C 55	02/11/1918	02/11/1918
War Diary	Bermerain Q 22a 44 (51A)	03/11/1918	03/11/1918
War Diary	Genlain L 23b 59 Sheet 57 A	04/11/1918	04/11/1918
War Diary	Warmes Le Petit G 34a 59 Sheet 51	05/11/1918	07/11/1918
War Diary	Bavay 9 25a 90 Sheet 51	08/11/1918	16/11/1918
War Diary	Jenlain (Valuei Esnes 1-100,000)	17/11/1918	17/11/1918
War Diary	Disy (Valuei Esnes 1-100,000)	18/11/1918	18/11/1918
War Diary	Somain	19/11/1918	25/11/1918
War Diary	Rumegies (Valueiesnes. 1-10000)	27/11/1918	30/11/1918
Heading	Dec 1918 No. 74 F. A.		
War Diary	Gruson (Sheet 3) 1-40000	01/12/1918	16/12/1918
War Diary	M. 33 Centers	17/12/1918	31/12/1918
Heading	24th Div Jan 1919 No 74 Field Ambulance		
War Diary	Gruson (Sheet 37 M 33 Central)	01/01/1919	31/01/1919
Heading	Feb 1919 No 74 Field Ambulance		
War Diary	Gruson (Sheet 37 M 33 Central)	01/02/1919	28/02/1919
Heading	Mar 1919 74th F.A.		
War Diary	Gruson (Sheet 37 M 33 Central)	01/03/1919	31/03/1919
Heading	Apr 1919 74th F.A.		
War Diary	Gruson M. 33 Central Sh 37 Belgium report of France.	01/04/1919	30/04/1919
War Diary	May 1919 No 74 Field Ambulance		
War Diary	Gruson M 33. Central Sheet 37. Belgium Part Of France	01/05/1919	15/05/1919
War Diary	Gruson Sheet 37 (M 33 Central)	16/05/1919	31/05/1919

WO/95/2202/3
74 Field Ambulance

24TH DIVISION
MEDICAL

74TH FLD AMBULANCE
AUG 1915 - DEC 1918
1919 MAY

24TH DIVISION
MEDICAL

24th D

24th Division
74th 93. Bde.

Summarised Vol I

12/7678

Aug 6. Oct 15
Dec 15

Aug.
S. Lewis 1915
Sept

Army Form C. 2118

Instructions regarding War Diaries and Intelligence
Summaries are contained in F.S. Regs., Part II.
and the Staff Manual respectively. Title pages
will be prepared in manuscript.

WAR DIARY 74th Field Ambulance
or
INTELLIGENCE SUMMARY. 24th Division

(Erase heading not required.)

Place	Date	Hour	Summary of Events and Information	Remarks and references to Appendices
EASTBOURNE	21.8.15		Unit engaged in Field Ambulance training - special attention paid to collection of wounded under fire "conditions" - heavy gale, without sunshine -	Mr Rice Capt a name
"	22.8.16		Sunday - Divine service 11 am	Jm R
EASTBOURNE	23.8.15		Final Inspection by Lt Col. Beagle R.A.M.C. Commanding Training centre arriving at 10.30 am arriving at BROOKWOOD at 1.30 - Behaviour and march via PIRBRIGHT to BULLSWATER CAMP. -	Jm R
BULLSWATER	24.8.15		Unit engaged in Drill and General Training. Also arranging 1st drawing of Ordinance Equipment from store - Horses already arrived	Jm R
"	25.8.15		Part of Ordnance Equipment of A. Sec received - training at to RPC action fitting of men with overseas boots etc. - 18 Mules arrived	Jm R
"	26.8.15		Inoculation of 45 men to be protected for receipt of Corps pay - new equipment - Horses inoculated - medical -	Jm R
"	27.8.15		Further issue of Equipment to men - also clothing - men inoculated again Lecture	Jm R
"	28.8.15		Distribution of Equipment - Lecture to N.C.O. in medical & Surgical Panniers	M. R
"	29.8.15		Sunday	
"	30.8.15		Practicing loading and unloading of Equipment. Fitting of harness to horses & mules.	M R

WAR DIARY or INTELLIGENCE SUMMARY

Army Form C. 2118

No. 1 Field Ambulance
94th Division

Place	Date	Hour	Summary of Events and Information	Remarks and references to Appendices
BULSWATER	31.8.15		Further practice [in] loading and unloading Equipment - biscuit fires.	M.R
BULSWATER	1.9.15		Left BULSWATER in two detachments for FARBRIGHT Station entraining at 11am & 1pm - arriving at SOUTHAMPTON at 1pm and 3pm - Advance - the horses & its limits embarked on the H.M.T. EMPRESS QUEEN and the horses and transport on H.M.T. NIAGARA	M.R
SOUTHAMPTON			Left SOUTHAMPTON at 6 pm arriving at HAVRE 2.30 am 2.9.15 - Sea rough and wet night -	M.R
HAVRE	2.9.15		Disembarked at HAVRE at 7am - Marched to Camp V arriving there at 12 noon - Officers and men in tents - Weather fine but rain cloudy.	M.R
HAVRE	3.9.15		Left V. at early [morning] at 7.30am and entrained at Gare des Marchandises Point 3. at 8.30am - Route via ABBEVILLE and MONTRAILLIER-BUCHY	M.R
MARESQUEL	4.9.15		Arrived here at 1.30 am and detrained. Marched at 5 am to NEUVILLE-SOUS-MONTREUIL arriving at 12 noon - Day bright & clear - Men carried fresh meat & biscuits	M.R
NEUVILLE SOUS MONTR.	5.9.15		Sunday - Divine Service at 4 pm -	M.R
NEUVILLE	6.9.15		Packing the ambulance wait - Received orders that at 2.30 pm visit the MARLES, MARENLA, LOISON, and adjoining LEBIEZ at 7.30 for beautiful billets - Men arrived hot and cheerful a few men fell out on the march & taken 4. - weather very fine, brilliant sunshine	M.R

Army Form C. 2118

WAR DIARY
or
INTELLIGENCE SUMMARY.
(Erase heading not required.)

74th Field Ambulance
24th Division

Place	Date	Hour	Summary of Events and Information	Remarks and references to Appendices
LEBIEZ	7.9.15		Arranging sanitary arrangements etc. Matters in hand — Some trifles indisposition only to prevent mens help etc —	Sh.R.
LEBIEZ	8.9.15		Inspection by D. Gen. Statius and Maj Gen Sir J. Ramsay — Allotted necessary in matters of flying horse and encampment of horse lines —	Ack.
LEBIEZ	9.9.15		Moving of cookhouses and latrines to heightening field — Pitching of Ambulance Camp weather fine brilliant sunshine — flies very troublesome also Wasps Multiple	Sh.R.
LEBIEZ	10.9.15		Movement of men for limits clothing — Lecture to Officers in the use of Gas Helmets, took for OC Dist Str 11th Corps — Pitching field Ambulance Encampment.	Sh.R.
LEBIEZ	11.9.15		Tactical Exercise with Division near EMERY - RIMBOVAL - reach Brigades — Same dressing station formed — Return to Camp 8pm — More sandal (Orthopedic) arrived.	Sh.R.
LEBIEZ	12.9.15		Sunday — Divine Service 11 am —	
LEBIEZ	13.9.15		All section exercised at Field Ambulance work — Visit from ADMS 24th Division — Health good — Brilliant sunshine — flies very numerous.	Sh.R.
LEBIEZ	14.9.15		Lecture scheme but Brenais — Rain — Storms abundant — Route march Subalterns as weather cleared — light rates — Arrangement of balls for men — also shower baths made from old biscuit tins inspected on line —	Sh.R.
LEBIEZ	15.9.15		All section training in collection of Casualties and formation of dressing stations — Health good — Deaths of troops good — No prevalent diseases —	Sh.R.

Army Form C. 211

4

74th Field Ambulance
24th Division

WAR DIARY
or
INTELLIGENCE SUMMARY.
(Erase heading not required.)

Instructions regarding War Diaries and Intelligence Summaries are contained in F.S. Regs., Part II. and the Staff Manual respectively. Title pages will be prepared in manuscript.

Place	Date	Hour	Summary of Events and Information	Remarks and references to Appendices
LEBIEZ	16.9.15		Unit engaged in Route March – distance 9 miles – New feet – been another boiling pancake – heavy rain – clouds of dust in billets – Clientele of him fairly illness – Medical known in use of Sar Melanie. God – No prevailing illness – Unit engaged in Field Ambulance work – Medical times by Lt Clarke in Anatomy and Physiology	Ap.P.
LEBIEZ	17.9.15			Ap.R.
LEBIEZ	18.9.15		Unit engaged in tactical scheme with Division – Marched out at 4 am – Operation commenced at 4.35 – moving in two Brigades – hot Gun Staffs – Dairy station formed and became ambulance sentiment direction of St HUMBERT – Shuttle turnkeys at 10 am – Arrived back at LEBIEZ as Casualty Collector – No casualties – Return from Field Ambulance at 11.30 –	Ap.L.
LEBIEZ	19.9.15		A and C. section marched off at 10.30 am Route via LOISON - OFFIN - MARESNES and MARLES arriving at NEUVILLE sous MONTREUIL at 4 pm – hundreds billets – B. section became ambulance at LEBIEZ to hand over to 73rd Field Ambulance	Ap.R.
NEUVILLE S. MONTREUIL	20.9.15		A+C section in bivouac moving out to billets in outskirts of Lorraine – hitherto marched also. Brown ambulance sent out at 2.30 pm to fetch collection of casualties but regular stretcher bearers of 71st Brigades – B. section ambulance from LEBIEZ at 6 pm -	Ap.R.
NEUVILLE	21.9.15		Inspection of boots, socks, shirts etc of unit – Clothing issues where necessary also socks – Reams orders through – Marched off at 3.30 p.m. – Route – via La Motte MANINGHEM - Pt. ST. MICHEL - MAISON CELLE - MONTEUILLE aus billets at Chateau du RADINGHEM. arriving 5 am 22.9.15 – Men tired but marched well.	

2353. Wt. W2544/1454 700,000 5/15 D.D. & L. A.D.S.S./Forms/C. 2118.

Army Form C. 2118

74 Fus Ambulance

Instructions regarding War Diaries and Intelligence Summaries are contained in F.S. Regs., Part II. and the Staff Manual respectively. Title pages will be prepared in manuscript.

WAR DIARY
or
INTELLIGENCE SUMMARY.
(Erase heading not required.)

Place	Date	Hour	Summary of Events and Information	Remarks and references to Appendices
RINDINGHEM	22.9.15	—	Left RODINGHEM at 6 pm. route via BOMY, ESTREE BLANCHE, MAZINGHEM, MIDLINGHEM, BERGUETTE in billets — heavy heat of Brigade fell out on march — Motor Ambulances & Motors was to pick up stragglers — arrived BERGUETTE at 5 am —	Nil
BERGUETTE	23.9.15		Men resting and washing — Left at 7 pm for LE CORNET BOURDOIS — 3½ kilometres distant — arrived 9 pm — went into billets — Rained heavily for 3 hours	Nil
LE CORNET	24.9.15		In billets — very damp. Slight showers at intervals — men cheerful — no prevailing disease. Left LE CORNET at 6.30 pm. in company with the rest of the Brigade & 2/AS 72 & 73. proceeded to BETHUNE.	Nil
BETHUNE	25.9.15	9.30 A.M	Arrived at 2AM. Men had early food. Transport parked inside CHAMPS de MARS. Men officers billeted nearby. Weather fine. Moonlight. Brigade moved out followed by Horse Ambulances of the 2 ABC Horse Ambulances towards VERMELLE (VERMELLE)	Nil
		2.30 PM	Tent subdivisions with Transport — horses moved — followed & halted to night at BEAUVRY. Very heavy rain set in afternoon. Heavy gun firing from direction of the shells LaBASSÉE. Many casualties tracking flying down. Cars passed our HQ.	
		8 PM.	Returns escaped to Brigade who established themselves for the night in a cellar at VERMELLES. They were under light-shell fire.	
BEAUVRY	26.9.15	9.30 am	Location fine. B Section tent Subdivision moved up to VERMELLES Dressing Station established in conjunction with a party from 72 F.A. Many casualties treated. ABC Section tent Subdivisions remained in reserve at BEAUVRY.	Nil
		8.PM.	Motor Ambulances despatched to dressing station at VERMELLE — Brigade in action — 6328. Pte Sloan + 6262 Pte Smith wounded	
BEAUVRY	27.9.15		A.B.C. Bearer Subdivisions Bgds in collecting wounded — heavy casualties —	Nil
			B. Bearer Subdivision searching for wounded in area of 7th Division out A.T.C. over 7th. Brigade area — B. Tent Subdivision at VERMELLES Dsg. Busy all night — Total number of casualties treated 300.	
BEAUVRY	28.9.15		Left BEAUVRY at 6.30 pm. Route via BETHUNG to ANNEZIN — heavy storm — arrived 11.30 pm — into billets	M.R.

Army Form C. 2118.

74th Field Ambulance

WAR DIARY
or
INTELLIGENCE SUMMARY.

(Erase heading not required.)

Place	Date	Hour	Summary of Events and Information	Remarks and references to Appendices
ANNEZIN.	29.9.15		Left ANNEZIN at 2.30 p.m. Heavy rain. Marched via CHOCQUES and LILLERS to BOURECQ arriving 5 p.m. into billets.	A.H.R.
~~ANNEZIN~~ BOURECQ.	30.9.15		In billets. Troops resting. General health good - no prevailing disease.	A.H.R.

A.H. Rose
Captain
O.C. 74th Field Ambulance

No. 74. 7. a.

Army Form C.2118

WAR DIARY
or
INTELLIGENCE SUMMARY.
(Erase heading not required.)

74th Field Ambulance
Capt Roe
Commanding

Place	Date	Hour	Summary of Events and Information	Remarks and references to Appendices
BOURECQ	1.10.15	—	In billets. Brigade resting – Weather temp good – no prevailing disease	AmRoe Capt RAMC Commanding
PROVEN	2.10.15	—	Left BOURECQ at 7am by road via HAM-EN-ARTOIS for BERGUETTE railway station and entrained men at 9.30 am. Transport proceeded by road – arrived at GODEWAERSWELDE at 11 am, detrained and marched via WATOU to billets 3 Huts of Château COURTHOVE in PROVEN arriving 1.30 pm – men accommodated in barns others in tents	AmR / AmR
PROVEN	3.10.15		Men resting – Divine Service 9 am – Day spent staining "lints" hut – "Kukel" – improving billets and sanitary arrangements –	AmR
PROVEN	4.10.15		Inspection of 74th Field Ambulance by G.O.C Division Maj Gen Capper	AmR
PROVEN	5.10.15		Brigade moved to 3rd Division area – 3rd Cavl. bivouacs at PROVEN.	AmR / AmR
HILLEHOEK	6.10.15		Field Ambulance moved via ABEELE to HILLEHOEK arriving 1 pm – (HAZEBROUCK 5A) Reports to 8th DRAG 3rd Division – at RENINGHELST – also to O.C. 8th Fd Ambulance at POPERINGHE for Instructions – locate – cool –	AmR
HILLEHOEK	7.10.15	7-10-15	Officers and men sent to 8th Fd Amb to receive instruction wounded in trench warfare – Weather cool – Sky cloudy Routine as on 7th – Issue of clothing to men of unit when required –	AmR
HILLEHOEK	8.10.15		Visit to C Amb – Battle Coes and chill – Sky cloudy	AmR

WAR DIARY
or
INTELLIGENCE SUMMARY

Army Form C. 2118

74th Field Ambulance

(Erase heading not required.)

Place	Date	Hour	Summary of Events and Information	Remarks and references to Appendices
HILLEHOEK	9.10.15		Officers sent for instruction to No 8 Fd Amb. – Weather dull – cold – no rain – All ranks supply of rations got from ABEELE twice daily from men as local supplies unavailable – Health of men good – No disease prevalent except scabies	Sh R
HILLEHOEK	10.10.15		Divine service 9.30 am – 2 Officers & NCO & 6 besides sent for instruction to Advanced Dressing Station No 8 Fd Ambulance	Sh R
BOESCHEPE	11.10.15		Staff Field Ambulance left HILLEHOEK at 3.30 pm via ABEELE arriving BOESCHEPE at 5 pm – Ambulance Rest Station from 72nd Fd Amb. taken over Officers and men in billets.	Sh R
BOESCHEPE	12.10.15		Arranged Hospital accommodate and making arrangements for taking over Divisional	Sh R
BOESCHEPE	13.10.15		Bathing of troops in hue thing. 240 men per day – took over A.D.S. Pais 74th Field Ambulance	Sh R
BOESCHEPE	14.10.15		All arrangements being carried out – took over charge of stables & self influes hygiene – at Boeschepe from 29th Field Ambulance – health men cloudly	Sh L
BOESCHEPE	15.10.15		Lecturing men some to affective attention. to DRS being Ambulance	Sh L
BOESCHEPE	16.10.15		Visit fm D.D.M.S. V Corps – Inspection of Hospitals and Billets	Sh L
BOESCHEPE	17.10.15		Visit of Inspection by Surg. Gen Porter, D.M.S. 2nd Army. – Divine Service 9.30 am – Inoculation the men of the Field Ambulance has been begun.	Sh B

Army Form C. 2118

WAR DIARY
or
INTELLIGENCE SUMMARY.

(Erase heading not required.)

74th Field Ambulance

Place	Date	Hour	Summary of Events and Information	Remarks and references to Appendices
BOESCHEPE	18.10.15		Patients at Hospitals and Billets continues — Latrines on the Separation System being constructed, also incineration etc. Weather cold and dry	M.u.R.
BOESCHEPE	19.10.15		Visit to A.D.M.S. re. Water supply for Baths for Troops of Division — all other work being continued — Weather cold and dry — Troops healthy —	M.u.R.
BOESCHEPE	20.10.15		Visit from A.D.M.S. 24th Division — Inspecting Hospital for self supporting quits — all work continued	M.u.B.
BOESCHEPE	21.10.15		Health of Troops good — weather cold and bright — nothing unusual to report.	M.u.R.
BOESCHEPE	22.10.15		Construction of new Cookhouse for billets continues —	M.u.R.
BOESCHEPE	23.10.15		Visit to A.D.M.S. — nothing unusual to report — Weather colder — no rain — Investigate of huts settling for Divisional Baths —	A.u.R.
BOESCHEPE	24.10.15		Divine Service 10.30 am — Weather good —	M.u.R. M.u.R.
BOESCHEPE	25.10.15		Heavy rain during the night and day — nothing unusual to report	M.u.R.
BOESCHEPE	26.10.15		Weather hot cold — Healthy Troops good — Certain amount of practice of latrine product.	M.u.R.
BOESCHEPE	27.10.15		Weather still wet cold — rain at intervals — roads very bad — 1 St. Sgt and four Privates sent at 6am to RENINGHELST to be located in Ennui as parade.	M.u.R.

Army Form C. 2118

WAR DIARY
or
INTELLIGENCE SUMMARY.
(Erase heading not required.)

74th Field Ambulance

Instructions regarding War Diaries and Intelligence Summaries are contained in F. S. Regs., Part II. and the Staff Manual respectively. Title pages will be prepared in manuscript.

Place	Date	Hour	Summary of Events and Information	Remarks and references to Appendices
BOESCHEPE	28.10.15		Weather very hot - Practice Estate Parade - aring hut - to train Sums	Ap 2
BOESCHEPE	29.10.15		Weather improving - Improvements in housing of men - Latrines - Wet & dry	Ap 2
			28 Aug	ready bath accommodation begun for patients
BOESCHEPE	30.10.15		Weather still improving - no rain - Stew Coys - Various improvements to Hospital	Ap 2
				and basis Stew Latrines - No prevailing disease among troops - Visit from
				Surg. 2nd Army -
BUESCHEPE	31.10.15		Weather cold - Divine Service 11.30 am -	

Aur Ros
Major RAMC
OC 74th Field Ambulance

74 Feb 2. a.
vol 3

121/7624

24th Museum

Nov. 15

Nov 1915

Army Form C. 2118

WAR DIARY
or
INTELLIGENCE SUMMARY

(Erase heading not required.)

74th Field Ambulance

Instructions regarding War Diaries and Intelligence Summaries are contained in F. S. Regs., Part II. and the Staff Manual respectively. Title pages will be prepared in manuscript.

Place	Date	Hour	Summary of Events and Information	Remarks and references to Appendices
BOESCHEPE	1.XI.15		Weather rather Cold and Cloudy – Some rain. Bronchial Catarrh very prevalent among officers and men of the Field Ambulance and troops	Much Rain major pains
BOESCHEPE	2.XI.15		Raining heavily – roads and fields very bad – Considerable interference with motor transport	Much R
BOESCHEPE	3.XI.15		Still raining and rather cold – Bronchial catarrh still prevalent also myalgia among troops – Visit to ADMS 24th Division	Much R
BOESCHEPE	4.XI.15		Weather improving – not so much rain – Still Cold – Inspection by him of Hospital for Self Inflicted Injuries.	Much R
BOESCHEPE	5.XI.15		No rain – roads still bad – Colder – Fire occurred in billet next to Mine occupied by No 20m. Inf. Reg. Works – no casualties	Much R
BOESCHEPE	6.XI.15		Weather improving – no rain – rather Cold – Bus diseases prevalent	Much R
BOESCHEPE	7.XI.15		Weather improving – nothing unusual to report.	Mud Mu R
BOESCHEPE	8.XI.15		Weather Cold – no prevailing disease	Mud Mu R
BOESCHEPE	9.XI.15		Visit from ADMS 24th Division – Inspection of Hospital – Weather Cold. Some rain	Mud
BOESCHEPE	10.XI.15		Weather Clearer – no rain – rather Cold – Wind high – Paris Rouen.	Mud

Army Form C. 2118
12

WAR DIARY
or
INTELLIGENCE SUMMARY.

(Erase heading not required.)

7th Field Ambulance

Instructions regarding War Diaries and Intelligence Summaries are contained in F. S. Regs., Part II. and the Staff Manual respectively. Title pages will be prepared in manuscript.

Place	Date	Hour	Summary of Events and Information	Remarks and references to Appendices
BOESCHEPE	11.XI.15	—	No rain – Moderately cold – Nothing unusual to report –	A.M.R.
BOESCHEPE	12.XI.15		Heavy rain all day – Not cold – Visit to A.D.M.S. 24th Division – No prevailing disease.	A.M.R.
BOESCHEPE	13.XI.15		Heavy rain – Wind very high – Moderately cold –	A.M.R.
BOESCHEPE	14.XI.15		Brig. Moderately cold – Inspection of Divisional Rest Station by Maj. Gen. Capper G.O.C. 24th Division and D.D.M.S. Burwell A.D.M.S. 24th Division – Divine service 10.30 a.m. –	M.R.
BOESCHEPE	15.XI.15		Cold and dry – Nothing unusual to report.	M.R.
BOESCHEPE	16.XI.15		Slight showers at intervals – Moderately cold – No prevailing disease	M.R.
BOESCHEPE	17.XI.15		Moderately cold and damp – Some sunshine – Nothing unusual to report	M.R.
BOESCHEPE	18.XI.15		Lecture by Surg. Gen. Sir Anthony Bowlby to Medical Officers of 5th Corps at BOESCHEPE 10 am – Weather cold –	M.R.
BOESCHEPE	19.XI.15		Weather cold and dry – No invading disease.	M.R.
BOESCHEPE	20.XI.15		Visit to A.D.M.S. 24th Division – Received orders to hand over to No. 8 Field Ambulance 24th Division moving out from Trenches.	M.R.
BOESCHEPE	21.XI.15		Preparation for handing over Divisional Rest Station, Baths and Hospital for Septic & Medical Injuries –	A.M.R.

Army Form C. 2118
13

WAR DIARY or INTELLIGENCE SUMMARY.

74th Field Ambulance.

(Erase heading not required.)

Place	Date	Hour	Summary of Events and Information	Remarks and references to Appendices
BOESCHEPE	22.XI.15	—	Preparing for departure – Handing over to 88th Field Ambulance –	Sh. McRose Major/Maine
		5 p.m.	Left BOESCHEPE – route via GODWAERSWELDE to EECKE arriving 7 p.m. 2 hrs. night dry and cold – brilliant moonlight – very frosty. Horses picketed in the open –	
EECKE	23.XI.15		Field Ambulance – resting in billets – a few sick from 17th Inf. Brigade sent to hospital at HAZEBROUCK by Field Ambulances –	Jn. R.
OEHTEZEELE	24.XI.15		Left EECKE at 10.30 a.m. route via St SYLVESTRE CAPPEL – CASSEL arriving OEHTEZEELE at 3.30 p.m. – day cool, pleasantly cold – horses billeted 5 p.m. – very few stragglers from 17th Brigade – Officers and men in billets, horses in open.	Jn. R.
HOULLE	25.XI.15		Left OEHTEZEELE at 11 a.m. route via Le MENEGAT – BAZEMBERG – WATTEN to HOULLE. Arriving at 4.30 p.m. – Officers and men in billets, horses in open fields – very few sick from 17th Brigade – about 19 footsore men carried in horse ambulances to their destination.	Jn. R.
CHATEAU DE LA VIERGETTE (EPERLEQUES)	26.XI.15		Left HOULLE at 10.30 a.m. route via HELLEBROUCK – EPERLEQUES to CHATEAU DE LA VIERGETTE. ½ mile N.W. of EPERLEQUES. – All Officers and men billeted in the Chateau, all horses in Stables – Reinforcement of 1 Offr and 7 transport Arrived and posted to Section	Jn. R.

Army Form C. 2118

WAR DIARY or INTELLIGENCE SUMMARY

74th Field Ambulance

(Erase heading not required.)

Place	Date	Hour	Summary of Events and Information	Remarks and references to Appendices
CHATEAU DE LA VIERGETTE	27.XI.15		Rearrangement of fields - and distribution of work in Unit - Portion of Chateau Vierqette converted to Hospital - Collection of Sick from Brigade Area - Arranges -	A.R.
H. de la V.	28.XI.15		Improvements to billets - cubicles - Visit from G.O.C. 17th Inf. Brigade - Weather very cold - Cleansing of transport wagons -	A.R.
H. de la V.	29.XI.15		Inspection by G.O.C. 24th Division - Weather cold - trolly - Return of T. Wagons etc. - Additional blankets got for men Sent -	A.R.
H. de la V.	30.XI.15		Weather milder - Some sunshine - Lt. Burnie to 3rd Rifle Brigade for temporary duty - Sgt Major Hotham + 1 man A.S.C. on 8 days leave to England.	A.R.

A.R. Rose
Major R.A.M.C.
O.C. 74th Field Ambulance

Dec. 1915

24th Div.

74th F.A.
vol: 3

74th F. A.

121/7910

Army Form C. 2118.

WAR DIARY
or
INTELLIGENCE SUMMARY.

(Erase heading not required.)

74th Field Ambulance 15

Instructions regarding War Diaries and Intelligence
Summaries are contained in F. S. Regs., Part II.
and the Staff Manual respectively. Title pages
will be prepared in manuscript.

Place	Date	Hour	Summary of Events and Information	Remarks and references to Appendices
CHATEAU DE LA VIERGETTE (EPERLEQUES)	1.XII.15	—	Weather bright – Sunshine – not cold – Route march – General fatigues	Au.R. Major Rainy
Ch. de la V.	2.XII.15		Sunshine – weather mild, rather damp – No prevailing disease – Officers 73rd Bac. Steps to hear lecture on Anti-Gas measures.	Au.R.
Ch. de la V.	3.XII.15		Weather very wet – no prevailing disease – Construction of wash house for men proceeds with also other improvements entailed. –	Au.R.
Ch. de la V.	4.XII.15		1 N.C.O. and 7 men of the draft recently arrived placed in isolation in account of the occurrence of measles of Cruke – Special Hospital amongst Annie's draft which joined 73rd Field Ambulance. – Three men from Westrich in Hosp. 26.3.	Mu.R.
Ch.de la V.	5.XII.15		Service G.20 a.m. – weather mild – some rain –	Mu.R.
Ch. de la V.	6.XII.16		Very wet – and windy – heavy rain during the night – the	Mu.R. Much
Ch. de la V.	7.XII.15		N.C.O. and men mentioned above taken out of quarantine. Lt. DUNCAN on leave. weather rather wet and cold – men leave for Renti march – Influenza prevalent among troops – a few cases of Neuralgia in hospital.	Mu.R.
Ch. de la V.	8.XII.15			Mu.R.
Ch. de la V.	9.XII.15		Cold and damp. Lt. HUXTABLE to temporary duty with 2nd Lincoln Regt.	Mu.R.

Army Form C. 2118.

WAR DIARY
or
INTELLIGENCE SUMMARY.
(Erase heading not required.)

74th Field Ambulance

Place	Date	Hour	Summary of Events and Information	Remarks and references to Appendices
H. de la V.	10.XII.15		Weather hotter - nothing unusual to report - draft of 7 men arrived from ROUEN. Men in quarantine	AncR. trisigar.
H. de la V.	11.XII.15		Weather wet - am wind high - Lt CHANCE returned from leave 11th XII 15 -	AncR.
H. de la V.	12.XII.15		Heath improving - Divine Service 10.45 am	AncR / MuR.
H. de la V.	13.XII.15		No rain - Strand drying - nothing unusual exercise.	AnR / MuR.
H. de la V.	14.XII.15		Route march - Eight miles went to St. MARTIN - OUX - LAERTES w Divelange	MuR
H. de la V.	15.XII.15		Nothing unusual to report - Heather cuts and drug - Lt DUNCAN return fm leave	MuR
H. de la V.	16.XII.15		Weather rather damp - nothing unusual exercise	MuR
H. de la V.	17.XII.15		Lt JOHNSTON to 8th BUFFS for temporary duty -	MuR
H. de la V.	18.XII.15		Lt HUXTABLE rejoined unit fm temporary duty with Lt: Kinder Regt. Lt SOUTHEY rejoined unit fm temporary duty with 12th R. FUSILIERS.	AncR
H. de la V.	19.XII.15		Divine Service 10.45 am -	MuR
H. de la V.	20.XII.15		Weather rather hot - nothing unusual to report.	MueR

Army Form C. 2118.

WAR DIARY
or
INTELLIGENCE SUMMARY.

(Erase heading not required.)

74th Field Ambulance 17

Place	Date	Hour	Summary of Events and Information	Remarks and references to Appendices
Clude la VIERGETTE	21.XII.15		Weather demp. Nothing unusual to report. Pais 74th Field Amb.	AMcRoss Major
Chdela V.	22.XII.15		Weather wet - not cold - Route march - no marching distance	MR
Chdela V.	23.XII.15		Some sunshine - no rain - not cold -	MR
Chdela V.	24.XII.15		Conference with A.D.M.S. 24th Division	MR
Chdela V.	25.XII.15		Christmas Day - Divine Service 11 a.m. - Weather fair.	MR
Chdela V.	26.XII.15		Nothing unusual to report - weather fair - Divine Service 11 a.m.	AMcR
Chdela V.	27.XII.15		Nothing unusual to report.	MR
Chdela V.	28.XII.15		Visit from A.D.M.S. 24th Division - Inspection of Billets	MR
Chdela V.	29.XII.15		Weather turning good - no rain -	MR
Chdela V.	30.XII.15		Nothing unusual to report - no marching distance	AMcR
Chdela V.	31.XII.15		Inspection of Personnel & Field by G.O.C. 24th Division to POPERINGHE to march new billets	MR

AMcRose Major RAMC
OC 74" Field Ambulance

1/4 in 7a.
Vol: 4

24 th Dw

F/171/11

714 F-A

Jan. 1916

5

Army Form C. 2118.

/8

WAR DIARY
or
INTELLIGENCE SUMMARY.

74th Field Ambulance

(Erase heading not required.)

Instructions regarding War Diaries and Intelligence Summaries are contained in F.S. Regs., Part II. and the Staff Manual respectively. Title pages will be prepared in manuscript.

Place	Date	Hour	Summary of Events and Information	Remarks and references to Appendices
CH. DE LA VIERGETTE WESTROYE	1.1.16		New Years Day - weather fair - but very windy - no rain.	Au Rose map AuR. AuR.
Cle La V.	2.1.16		To see ADMS. re - new billets.	
Cle La V.	3.1.16		Jackie began to prepare for move - Exercich of Sick in Hospital - weather fair - some sunshine.	AuR
Cle de la V.	4.1.16		All transport and A.S.C. Personnel left by road today - route via NOORDPEENE and STEENVOORDE	Au R
Cle de la V.	5.1.16		Advance Party from 74th Fd Amb. Consisting of 2 Officers & 16 other ranks left by Cov for next billeting area.	Mul.
Cle de la V.	6.1.16		Advance Party from 53rd Fd Amb. arrived - Preparation for departure continued - Left billet at midnight 6th - Marched via ESTMONT and POLINCOVE to AUBRICQ Station and entrained at 4:30 am on 7th.	MulR
POPERINGHE	7.1.16		Arrived QUINTIN STATIN at 8:30am. detail'n marched via POPERINGE to new billet Situate 1 mile from POPERINGHE on the RENINGHELST Road.	JmR
POPERINGHE	8.1.16		Weather fair - no rain - taking over Camp from 53rd Field Ambulance.	Mul
POPERINGHE	9.1.16		Extensive cleaning up of Camp.	Mul
POPERINGHE	10.1.16		Attended Scout concert and - Industry for huts for men as present accomodation in barn leaves much to be desired.	Mul

Army Form C. 2118.

WAR DIARY
or
INTELLIGENCE SUMMARY.
(Erase heading not required.)

74 Field Ambulance 19.

Place	Date	Hour	Summary of Events and Information	Remarks and references to Appendices
POPERINGHE	11.1.16		Major Rose departed on leave. At 10 a.m. G.O.C. accompanied by D.H.O. and visited the camp. He approved of the plans for improvements made. Some suggestion regarding the drawing of the Field Paid Ambulance.	Nil
POPERINGHE	12.1.16		Lt. Col. MERRYMAN returned from leave. Lt. SOUTHEY proceeded to KRUISSTRAAT to relieve Lt. MACDONALD JOHNSTON who have completed seven days duty there. Visited N.C.O.s who began work for timber hunting-scheme. Visited C.R.E. who is to send an officer tomorrow. Camp will arrive to starting hut etc.	Nil
POPERINGHE	13.1.16		"Hutting Officer" Lt. WILLIAMS R.E. inspected camp. He agreed to build at least 10 huts to accommodate personnel. A kitchen, & a drying room. Later if possible he will erect a number of hut latrines wash house.	Nil
POPERINGHE	14.1.16		General cleaning, drawing, preparing report of the camp has been in continuous progress for the last 3 days. Previous supplies of bricks & barbed wire & being provided by the R.E's & Divisional R.E. return pioneers are now attached & no materials are arriving. The new huts have been indicated.	Nil
POPERINGHE	15.1.16		Been revised scheme for conducting Parade, using horse ambulances instead of functions is working satisfactorily. Requested M.O.i/c still make unreasonable demands for ambulances except hours but they are being informed gradually as to the Executive from these sick park. The grade will have an entry in need of repair.	Nil
POPERINGHE	16.1.16		The whole field ambulance was bathed at Divisional Baths between 10.30 a.m. midday. Church of England service in the afternoon.	Nil
POPERINGHE	17.1.16		Lieut. S.R. JOHNSTON appointed acting Div. SANITARY OFFICER with place of Lieut. CARRUTHERS on leave.	Nil
POPERINGHE	18.1.16		Every uneventful day. Visiting of patients proceeded for the present.	Nil
POPERINGHE	19.1.16		Clear bright day. Several enemy aeroplanes hovering the camp. Between 11.30 to 1.30 there was a bombardment of the field adjoining us on the WEST. 45 shells came over. Midway a fragment fell near the officers mess. No damage was done.	Nil
POPERINGHE	20.1.16		Major ROSE returned from leave. L. McGUARICH returned from temporary duty with DIVISIONAL TRAIN.	Nil

Army Form C. 2118.

WAR DIARY
or
INTELLIGENCE SUMMARY.

74th Field Ambulance 20

(Erase heading not required.)

Instructions regarding War Diaries and Intelligence Summaries are contained in F. S. Regs., Part II. and the Staff Manual respectively. Title pages will be prepared in manuscript.

Place	Date	Hour	Summary of Events and Information	Remarks and references to Appendices
POPERINGHE	21.1.16		Hutting general work in camp continues. Visited "Labour Battalion" hutt on OUDERDOM - VLAMETINGHE road which are staffed by our men. It is proposed to put an officer in charge largely increase the capacity of the baths.	MR
POPERINGHE	22.1.16		Visit from DMS 5th Corps. - Candidates of hutting and funeral camp improvements continued. - Lt HUXTABLE left to take over charge of Labour Batt. Baths.	MR
POPERINGHE	23.1.16		Divine Service 9.30 am. - Saw ruins of German aeroplane crashes some trees in the vicinity of the camp - no casualties.	MR
POPERINGHE	24.1.16		Weather fine - Hutting construction etc continues.	MR
POPERINGHE	25.1.16		Weather rather dull. All in movements continues - Lt McCURDICH returns leave	ThR
POPERINGHE	26.1.16		Visit from ADMS 24th Division. - Weather dull - foggy - cold	ThR
POPERINGHE	27.1.16		Hutting increase to report.	ThR
POPERINGHE	28.1.16		Weather still dull and foggy - heavy gun firing daily - no divisional movement during turns - all camp improvements continues.	ThR
POPERINGHE	29.1.16		Owing to shortage of working material we have commenced to dig a well - weather lighter.	MR
POPERINGHE	30.1.16		Sunday Divine Service - 10.30 am.	MR
POPERINGHE	31.1.16		Camp improvements continues - weather cold foggy.	ThR

A McRae
Major RAMC
OC 74th Field Ambulance

Feb 1916 —
74th Field Ambulance

74 Th. 7. a.
 vol: 5

Army Form C. 2118.

WAR DIARY
or
INTELLIGENCE SUMMARY. 74th Field Ambulance. 21.
(Erase heading not required.)

Instructions regarding War Diaries and Intelligence Summaries are contained in F. S. Regs., Part II. and the Staff Manual respectively. Title pages will be prepared in manuscript.

Place	Date	Hour	Summary of Events and Information	Remarks and references to Appendices
POPERINGHE	1.2.16		Visit from ADMS. 24th Division – weather bright – heavy firing most of the day	AMcR. Appendix
POPERINGHE	2.2.16		Weather still bright – some sunshine – 2 Coys moved to 2nd Div Train	AMcR.
POPERINGHE	3.2.16		Weather fair – all improvements carried out	AMcR.
POPERINGHE	4.2.16		Visit from GOC 24th Division – inspected Camp – no casualties	AMcR.
POPERINGHE	5.2.16		Advanced Dressing Station heavy shells – no casualties	AMcR.
POPERINGHE	6.2.16		Sunday – Divine Service at 11.30 a.m. – some rain	AMcR.
POPERINGHE	7.2.16		Day clear – cold – German aeroplanes dropped bombs in vicinity of Camp – no casualties	AMcR.
POPERINGHE	8.2.16		Visit from ADMS 24th Division – weather day cold – working unusual to Report	AMcR.
POPERINGHE	9.2.16		Day bright clear – cold – many aeroplane movements – unusual amount to Report	AMcR.

Army Form C. 2118.

WAR DIARY
or
INTELLIGENCE SUMMARY.

(Erase heading not required.)

N4. Field Ambulance 22.

Place	Date	Hour	Summary of Events and Information	Remarks and references to Appendices
POPERINGHE	10.2.16		Section of POPERINGHE been heavy shelled by hr during at 5.30 am and 7.30 pm. Walked Clean no early Cases -	Mr Rose hospitalis
POPERINGHE	11.2.16		Weather very Cold and wet. - Visit from CRE. 5th Corps - Inspection of Camp - took a bus to Motored addition -	J M R
POPERINGHE	12.2.16		Weather cold & fairly Clean - Public Gun ry lectures all day. German aeroplani dropped bombs in vicinity of Camp - Since Shelling of POPERINGE by Germans long-range guns - warned by ADMS at 5 pm "Gas alert". Scheme in lectures 30/pers 16 men was slatched for reinforcing 72 F.A. advanced dressing Station - Continued at 8 pm.	J M R
POPERINGHE	13.2.16		Were received from ADMS at 5 am at 6.15 pm - ordering 2 NCO & 50 other ranks but 15 Stretcher to proceed by bus to the Croyden YPRES. and from there to the Mill on the MENIN Road. to assist in the collection of Wounded - Lts Duncan & Dunmere were detailed to take w party at 6.30 am and collected wounded as far up as advanced line of British Trench. Under very heavy Shell, machine gun & rifle fire - one NCO and four men were wounded - one man suffered from "Shell shock."	J M R

Army Form C. 2118.

WAR DIARY
or
INTELLIGENCE SUMMARY.

(Erase heading not required.)

74th FIELD AMBULANCE.   23

Instructions regarding War Diaries and Intelligence Summaries are contained in F. S. Regs., Part II. and the Staff Manual respectively. Title pages will be prepared in manuscript.

Place	Date	Hour	Summary of Events and Information	Remarks and references to Appendices
Outteau	13.2.16		All wounded chiefly of 3rd Rifle Brigade were brought in — weather hot and windy — cold.	AWR Hughes
POPERINGHE	14.2.16		Alone meeting being arranged began at 11 a.m. — Weather windy — bell tolled — Received notification from ADMS 24th Divis. "Rheitoli" at 2 p.m. — lecture cancelled.	AWR
POPERINGHE	15.2.16		Weather cold and windy — Latin med. officers and Portuguese aeroplane have arrived over Dunton lines — Heavy gun fire in direction of YPRES been held in evening — high wing cold as winter. Visit from ADMS 24th Division. Gale blowing — with rain at intervals.	AWR / AWR
POPERINGHE	16.2.16			AWR
POPERINGHE	17.2.16		Visit from ADMS 24th Division — day dry cold — during the night a Zeppelin dropped bombs in POPERINGHE and vicinity — about 18 bombs in all —	AWR
Poperinghe	18.2.16		At 8.30 a.m. three German aeroplanes came over flying low — dropped three bombs over REMY SIDING — weather dull and cloudy, some rain.	AWR

2353 Wt. W2544/1454 700,000 5/15 D. D. & L.   A.D.S.S./Forms/C. 2118.

Army Form C. 2118.

WAR DIARY
or
INTELLIGENCE SUMMARY.

(Erase heading not required.)

Instructions regarding War Diaries and Intelligence Summaries are contained in F. S. Regs., Part II. and the Staff Manual respectively. Title pages will be prepared in manuscript.

74 Field Ambulance 24

Place	Date	Hour	Summary of Events and Information	Remarks and references to Appendices
POPERINGHE	19.2.16	—	Bay fine clear — 1 Sgt and 5 men reinforcement arrived — 7 oc last —	Fine Rose keeps
POPERINGHE	20.2.16	—	Brilliant Sunshine — several German aeroplanes in trench of camp — at 7.30 a.m. — At 11 a.m. several bombs were dropped by hostile aircraft on POPERINGHE	Fine Rose keeps Mud Rose
POPERINGHE	21.2.16	—	Cold and wet — sky cloudy —	Mud Rose
POPERINGHE	22.2.16	—	Very cold — about 2 inches of snow on ground — Hostile aeroplane dropped bombs on POPERINGHE about midnight — Heavy firing by hostile guns aeroplane — Some gas shells dropped by enemy at our advanced dressing station at KRUISTRAAT.	Fine Rose Mud Mud
POPERINGHE	23.2.16	—	Cold and dry — snow — frost — freezing — Enemy aeroplane dropped 14 bombs in POPERINGHE at 9 a.m. —	Mud
POPERINGHE	24.2.16	—	Cold and dry — snow still on ground — brilliant sunshine — at noon enemy aeroplane dropped 3 bombs on POPERINGHE.	Mud Mud
POPERINGHE	25.2.16	—	Very cold and dull — no hostile aircraft — 1 man hostile enemy bombing over REMY HELST.	Mud Mud

Army Form C. 2118.

WAR DIARY
or
INTELLIGENCE SUMMARY.

(Erase heading not required.)

74th Field Ambulance. No. 25.

Place	Date	Hour	Summary of Events and Information	Remarks and references to Appendices
No. POPERINGHE	26.2.16		Cold and wet - tune spent towards evening in preventing draining. -	Mr Rae hospital Lieut R The R
No. POPERINGHE	27.2.16		Cold and wet - snow still lying - skies overcast - nothing unusual - dull weather - very little aeroplane activity.	
POPERINGHE	28.2.16		Cold and dull weather - to 10 C.C.S. degrees Pyrexia N.Y.D. Lieut Duncan R.A.M.C.	
POPERINGHE	29.2.16		Morning bright + clear - later chill and windy - Hostile aeroplane not very active - no prevailing sickness - heavy wind very good. -	

Arr Rae
Lt. Col. R.A.M.C.
OC 74th Field Ambulance.

74 J Amh
Vol 6

March 1916

Army Form C. 2118.

WAR DIARY
or
INTELLIGENCE SUMMARY.   74th Field Ambulance

(Erase heading not required.)

No. 26.

Place	Date	Hour	Summary of Events and Information	Remarks and references to Appendices
POPERINGHE	1.3.16		Day dull and cloudy - Some rain - Heavy British artillery fire during the night - Pte. WEAVIS. 13th Middlesex Regt. admitted suffering from Cerebro-Spinal Meningitis - transferred to 7.C.C.S. -	Fr. Rose Westeraw
POPERINGHE	2.3.16		Morning clear later cloudy - Some rain - Heavy firing by British guns all night - Nothing unusual to report	Shult
POPERINGHE	3.3.16		Morning dull & cloudy - Some rain - Nothing unusual to report.	Shul
POPERINGHE	4.3.16		Dull - Some Sunst - Weather cold - Very little hostile aircraft activity.	Shul
POPERINGHE	5.3.16		Divine Service 10.30 a.m. - Visit from C.R.E. 5th Corps - Weather cold - Some rain -	Shul
POPERINGHE	6.3.16		Visit from A.D.M.S. 24th Division - Sunst - Weather cold - Nothing unusual to report -	Shul
POPERINGHE	7.3.16		Sunst - rather cold - Nothing unusual to report	Shul

Army Form C. 2118.

WAR DIARY
or
INTELLIGENCE SUMMARY.   74th Field Ambulance

(Erase heading not required.)

27.

Instructions regarding War Diaries and Intelligence
Summaries are contained in F. S. Regs., Part II.
and the Staff Manual respectively. Title pages
will be prepared in manuscript.

Place	Date	Hour	Summary of Events and Information	Remarks and references to Appendices
POPERINGHE	8.3.16		Heavy showers during the night. - day bright & clear - Sunshine - our day much warmer.	McRae Dieppeine
POPERINGHE	9.3.16		Indian advanced & tabernacle advanced Dressing station at Méteren Café from 3rd Northumbrian Field Ambulance - took over 24 cases - Day clear and cool - from this lying in front - Athénée Café later over by 1 Officer & 20 Other ranks.	ShuR
POPERINGHE	10.3.16		Advanced Dressing station at KRUISTRAAT. handed over to 3rd Northumbrian Field Ambulance. - Day cool and dull. -	McR AuR
POPERINGHE	11.3.16		Day cold and dull - no sunshine - work to Arras & Sept Jerain.	LuR
POPERINGHE	12.3.16		Divine Service 10 a.m. - day rather cloudy & dull. - nothing unusual to report.	ShuR
POPERINGHE	13.3.16		Morning rather dull & cloudy. - later brilliant sunshine - very warm - visiting Irish mass during 5th Corps. -	McR
POPERINGHE	14.3.16		Morning clear and brilliant sunshine - later wind - Evening dull with rain.	McR

Army Form C. 2118.

WAR DIARY
or
INTELLIGENCE SUMMARY.
(Erase heading not required.)

4th Field Ambulance

28.

Instructions regarding War Diaries and Intelligence Summaries are contained in F. S. Regs., Part II. and the Staff Manual respectively. Title pages will be prepared in manuscript.

Place	Date	Hour	Summary of Events and Information	Remarks and references to Appendices
POPERINGHE	15.3.16	—	Weather mild - Sunshine - Visit from Brit. Gen. S.D. Corps - while returned Hospital - Considerable intake of Casualties, brought down from trenches Copse Adv. Dressing Station - during Afternoon.	McRae Lt.Col.
POPERINGHE	16.3.16		Visit from O.C. 3rd Canadian Division - day still moderate - Sanctuary Wood heavily shelled - casualties brought to trenches Copse Advance Dressing Station -	McR
POPERINGHE	17.3.16		Visit from OC 1st Canadian Fd Ambulance - locating bright relief -	McR
POPERINGHE	18.3.16		Day Clear and Milder - Our line - nothing unusual to report.	McR
POPERINGHE	19.3.16		Nothing unusual to report.	McR
POPERINGHE	20.3.16		Handed over A.D.S. at MAPLE COPSE to 5th Canadian Fd Ambulance	McR
BERTHEN	21.3.16		Newstown Camp R. 5th Canadian Fd Ambulance and marched off at 2 p.m. Route via RENINGHELST, HECKSEN, WESTOUTRE to BERTHEN - Men not billeted Nite - weather clear - muddy.	DeRue
BERTHEN	22.3.16		In billets - Transport horses in open - Visit from COUS 2nd Division - heavy rain clear - some rain	McR

2353 Wt. W2544/1454 700,000 5/15 D. D. & L. A.D.S.S./Forms/C. 2118.

Army Form C. 2118.

WAR DIARY
or
INTELLIGENCE SUMMARY. 74th Field Ambulance

(Erase heading not required.)

29

Place	Date	Hour	Summary of Events and Information	Remarks and references to Appendices
BERTHEN	23.3.16	-	Weather fairly bright, rather cold. - Visit to No. 2 Canadian Field Ambulance at BAILLEUL to enquiry taking over of Streets	Ambulance ireal
BERTHEN	24.3.16	-	Snowing - days cold - Nothing unusual to report	Snl
BERTHEN	25.3.16	-	Still Cold and wet - Route march in morning -	Snl
BERTHEN	26.3.16	-	Cold and wet - Divine Service 10 am -	Snl
BERTHEN	27.3.16	-	Visits - Advanced Dressing Station and Dressing Station of 2d Canadian Field Amb. and arranged taking over from them -	Snl
BERTHEN	28.3.16	-	Visit to ADMS 24th Division - Wounded Cold and rain high	Snl
BERTHEN	29.3.16	-	C. Section visits three Officers 10th and Advanced Dressing Station 1 mile north of PLOEGSTEERTE, and Dressing Station at ROMARIN, his no 2 Canadian Field Ambulance -	Mud
BAILLEUL	30.3.16	-	A.B. section left BERTHEN at 9 am and took over H.Q. from No 2 Canadian Field Ambulance at BAILLEUL	Snl
BAILLEUL	31.3.16	-	Visit to Adv Dressing Statn and Dressing 24th Division -	Ambulance Ambulance OC 74 Fd Amb

April 1916.

No. 74 F. Amb.

2nd Div.

COMMITTEE FOR THE
MEDICAL HISTORY OF THE WAR
Date   9 - JUN. 1915

Army Form C. 2118.

WAR DIARY or INTELLIGENCE SUMMARY.

(Erase heading not required.)

74th Field Ambulance. Vol 30

Place	Date	Hour	Summary of Events and Information	Remarks and references to Appendices
BAILLEUL	1.4.16	—	Weather bright & clear — brilliant sunshine — much warmer —	AW Pirie A/Col Pirie
BAILLEUL	2.4.16		Brilliant sunshine — warm day — visit to Dressing Station at ROMARIN.	MWJ
BAILLEUL	3.4.16		Heavy firing by British Guns during the night — Inspection at Headquarters and Dressing Station Commenced — heavy rain — brilliant sunshine. LIEUT. HUXTABLE left for England — Reprisals of aircraft — struck off strength	MWR
BAILLEUL	4.4.16		Weather dull and rather cold — LIEUT. MACKWOOD arrived and taken on strength. Artillery fire very active on both sides	TWJ MWJ
BAILLEUL	5.4.16		Weather brighter. Stu'rador Cols — visit to transport lines — Artillery active	MWR
BAILLEUL	6.4.16		Weather still rather cold and chill — Artillery active —	A/Col.R. MWJ
BAILLEUL	7.4.16		5th Corps to Dressing Station — visit to sie Cos — Some sunshine — visit to across 24 Division	MWJ MWJ
BAILLEUL	8.4.16		Weather still rather cold — Artillery fairly quiet	MWJ
BAILLEUL	9.4.16		Visit from G.O.C. 24th Division — weather bright. Divine service 9.30 am. Inspection of Transport by O.C. 24 Division	MWJ
BAILLEUL	10.4.16		Weather rather cold — fine sunshine — Inspection of Transport by O.C. 24 Division. Train fine baking 5th Corps.	MWJ

Army Form C. 2118.

WAR DIARY
or
INTELLIGENCE SUMMARY.

74 Field Ambulance

31.

(Erase heading not required.)

Place	Date	Hour	Summary of Events and Information	Remarks and references to Appendices
BAILLEUL	11.4.16		Inspection ration Collection — Nothing unusual to report — Evening hot curries.	Stryker Tcol
BAILLEUL	12.4.16		Sick Coes — Improvements in Headquarters Cubicles — Cookhouses finished — Building of dining room for patients cubicles —	Mul R
BAILLEUL	13.4.16		Visit ASC in Division — Inspecting Wards Transport lines — Visits heavy Sections at ROMARIN and Collecting Post in NEUVE EGLISE roads	Mul R Mul
BAILLEUL	14.4.16		Cold and rain at intervals. Wind high. — very few wounded admitted.	Mul
BAILLEUL	15.4.16		Improvements at Headquarters Cubicles — also at transport lines — weather Cold —	Mul
			has high sun rain, hail —	Mul
BAILLEUL	16.4.16		Weather dull and rather Cold — June rain towards evening — Visits to Dressing	Mul
			Station — Advanced Dressing station and Collecting Post —	
BAILLEUL	17.4.16		Weather Cold and dull — Wind high —	
BAILLEUL	18.4.16		Visit per Motor to Division — Interview with Genl — Visits Dressing	Mul R
			Station and Collecting Post —	
BAILLEUL	19.4.16		Day Cold and wet — Wind rather high — Sunshine at intervals — Visit from	Mul R
			Stones ∇ Corps —	
BAILLEUL	20.4.16		Weather improving — Cool towards evening —	Mul

Army Form C. 2118.

WAR DIARY
or
INTELLIGENCE SUMMARY.
(Erase heading not required.)

74 Field Ambulance   32.

Place	Date	Hour	Summary of Events and Information	Remarks and references to Appendices
BAILLEUL	21.4.16	—	Weather improving - some sunshine - warmer - visit of probable by Surgeon General Porter . D.M.S. 2nd Army .	Mr Roe ACT / Mr R.
BAILLEUL	22.4.16		Weather like rattier cold - nothing unusual	Mr R.
BAILLEUL	23.4.16		Considerable hostile air activity - weather close.	Mr R.
BAILLEUL	24.4.16		Enemy aeroplanes came over town at 4. a.m. as also at 2 pm also. No further fire close to Unit H.Q. - no casualties - 2 enemy aeroplanes reported destroyed by Anti-aircraft guns (?) . Brilliant sunshine . Weather warm + dry .	Mr R. / Mr R.
BAILLEUL	25.4.16		Nothing unusual to report . Weather - cloudless sky - brilliant sunshine - Enemy artillery active over front line	Mr R.
BAILLEUL	26.4.16		Weather still fine - visited Bessex Statn. Advanced Dressing Statn.	Mr R.
BAILLEUL	27.4.16		Our Artillery active on NEUVE EGLISE ROAD .	Mr R.
BAILLEUL	28.4.16		Weather very fine . Brilliant sunshine - visit by A.D.M.S. to Dressing Station at ROMARIN .	Mr R.

Army Form C. 2118.

WAR DIARY
or
INTELLIGENCE SUMMARY.

74ᵗʰ Field Ambulance

33.

(Erase heading not required.)

Place	Date	Hour	Summary of Events and Information	Remarks and references to Appendices
BAILLEUL	29.4.16		Weather very fine – Cloudless sky – warm –	MivRue Neuve.–
BAILLEUL	30.4.16		At 2 a.m. the smell of chlorine gas was very perceptible in the tation air in a few minutes became very marked – Gas alarm was given and all preparation made for arrival of patients – all available cars sent to ROMARIN Evacuate Walkers to Bailleul Cases if necessary. – Walker of Gases totalled 19 Gases and 47 wounded. – The left section seems to suffer most from the Gas as to lights & lectiv While our dressing station draws were heavily affected – he gas was however less violent at the advanced Dressing station & the Dressing station – The 19 gases patients arrived from WULVERGHEM church & the RE huts were slightly gassed in return	Mivh

MivRue
Neuve.
OC 74 Fies Ambl

24th Div

No. 74 F. Amb.

May 1916.

S

Army Form C. 2118.

Vol 38

WAR DIARY
or
INTELLIGENCE SUMMARY.

74th Field Ambulance

(Erase heading not required.)

Instructions regarding War Diaries and Intelligence Summaries are contained in F. S. Regs., Part II. and the Staff Manual respectively. Title pages will be prepared in manuscript.

Place	Date	Hour	Summary of Events and Information	Remarks and references to Appendices
BAILLEUL	1.5.16		Weather fine, brilliant sunshine. Dodds passing station ROMARIN, advance dressing Station HYDE PARK CORNER and Collecting Post on NEUVE EGLISE ROAD — Vicinity of AUBURNE LOOS. Collecting Post heavily shelled by Germans (at 12 noon and 1 o'clock). 1/5 Casualties — Visited ADMS 25 Division — Thunderstorm 8 pm.	AuRue LOOS
BAILLEUL	2.5.16		Weather dull and cold. Slow overcast. Some rain	M.i.R.
BAILLEUL	3.5.16		Weather good. Brilliant sunshine. Nothing unusual to report.	Mul
BAILLEUL	4.5.16		Weather slightly cloudy. Enemy aeroplane activity in morning.	
BAILLEUL	5.5.16		Weather fine in the morning but cloudy in the afternoon — very close & thundery. Enemy aeroplane activity in the morning. A.D.M.S. with D.A.D.M.S. & Maj Edwards held a medical Board in our orderly room today to examine men for permanent duty at the Base. Ammonia Capsules are now to be included in every Regt M.O.'s stores (reserve 100 Capsules).	(APBD)
BAILLEUL	6.5.16		Dull in the afternoon — some showers — but sunny in the afternoon. Less aeroplane activity. Visited Romarin (M.D.S.)	(APBD)
BAILLEUL	7.5.16		Very little aeroplane activity. Weather still blowery much cooler.	(APBD)
BAILLEUL	8.5.16		Lieut Col Moyston acting A.D.M.S. Weather showery & cold. No aeroplane activity. Artillery seems less active than usual.	(APBD)
BAILLEUL	9.5.16		Very wet all day. Very little aeroplane or artillery activity. Visited A.D.M.S	(APBD)

Army Form C. 2118.

WAR DIARY
or
INTELLIGENCE SUMMARY.

74th Field Ambulance

(Erase heading not required.)

Place	Date	Hour	Summary of Events and Information	Remarks and references to Appendices
BAILLEUL	10.V.16		Weather sunny but still cold. A little aeroplane activity at intervals during the day. Medical Board on LIEUT IRVEN, 3rd RIFLE BDE. for PERMANENT COMMISSION	O.9.B.R.
BAILLEUL	11.V.16		LIEUT DUNMERE relieves LIEUT McPHERSON at A.D.S. Weather dry but overcast for the greater part of the day. Some aeroplane activity. Visited A.D.M.S. who returned with me to inspect the ambulance headquarters. He expressed himself as pleased with everything.	O.9.B.R. O.9.B.R.
BAILLEUL	12.V.16		Some aeroplane activity. Weather clear during forenoon but cloudy in afternoon. Visit from Col FEAKES of No. 2.C.C.S.	O.9.B.R.
BAILLEUL	13.V.16		Very dull wet – no aeroplane activity.	O.9.B.R.
BAILLEUL	14.V.16		Very dull all day – no aeroplane activity. The M.O. at HYDE PARK CORNER reports heavy shelling there yesterday. LIEUT DUNMERE & 2 C.C.S. Referred (NYD).	M.v.R.
BAILLEUL	15.V.16		Dull some rain – LIEUT DUNMERE evacuates to Base – Lt. D.J. CLARK and Lt. L. WALTON joins unit – this day on duty	J.v.R / M.v.R
BAILLEUL	16.V.16		Weather fine – Sunshine – Invites Dressing Station as. Collecting Post	J.v.R
BAILLEUL	17.V.16		Weather fine – brilliant sunshine – "Gas alert" –	M.v.R
BAILLEUL	18.V.16		Weather fine – brilliant sunshine – Visit by A.D.M.S.	J.v.R
BAILLEUL	19.V.16		Weather brilliant – nothing unusual to report	J.v.R
BAILLEUL	20.V.16		Weather fine – cloudless sky –	J.v.R
BAILLEUL	21.V.16		Weather fine – aeroplanes active	M.v.R

Army Form C. 2118.

WAR DIARY
or
INTELLIGENCE SUMMARY.

74th Field Ambulance

(Erase heading not required.)

Instructions regarding War Diaries and Intelligence Summaries are contained in F. S. Regs., Part II. and the Staff Manual respectively. Title pages will be prepared in manuscript.

Place	Date	Hour	Summary of Events and Information	Remarks and references to Appendices
BAILLEUL	22.V.16		Brilliant sunshine - fifteen wounded arrived to A.D.S. - last night -	McR McR McR
BAILLEUL	23.V.16		Weather fine. Good - Nothing unusual to Report.	
BAILLEUL	24.V.16		Inspection by Maj. Gen. Cuthie, G.O.C. 24 Division. About 24 sick - gas alert.	McR
BAILLEUL	25.V.16		Quiet night - no wounded - Weather hot. overcast -	McR
BAILLEUL	26.V.16		Col/S. McDiarmid Rasine (SR.) Jones Smith from D.D.M.S. Lastnight. T. Dr. Clark left & join 12 C.C.S. in relief - Rain prevented 4 men arrived to Return.	McR
BAILLEUL	27.V.16		Weather cool - Showery cloudy. - Nothing unusual to Report.	McR
BAILLEUL	28.V.16		Visit to Hd. Qtr. Comp. and Advance Dressing Station and Divisional HQ - Considerable enemy aerial activity - weather miserable. 4 Sanitary left to England -	McR
BAILLEUL	29.V.16		Weather very hot. - Nothing unusual to Report -	McR
BAILLEUL	30.V.16		Weather fine - very little enemy aerial activity - Three wounded during night from nightraiders -	McR
BAILLEUL	31.V.16		Lt. JOHNSTON R.A.M.C. left to England on seven days furlough - Nothing unusual to Report.	McR

McRae
War Name
O.C. 74 Field Ambulance

June 1916.

C16. 74 7.a.

COMMITTEE FOR THE
MEDICAL HISTORY OF THE WAR
Date 5 AUG 1915

Army Form C. 2118.

WAR DIARY
or
INTELLIGENCE SUMMARY.

(Erase heading not required.)

2¼" Field Ambulance Vol 9 No 37

Instructions regarding War Diaries and Intelligence Summaries are contained in F. S. Regs., Part II. and the Staff Manual respectively. Title pages will be prepared in manuscript.

Place	Date	Hour	Summary of Events and Information	Remarks and references to Appendices
BAILLEUL	1.6.15		Weather colder - less aerial activity - nothing unusual to report	App Rose store
BAILLEUL	2.6.15		Weather bright. Sunshine. Conductor aways of heavy firing early on sector. - Lecture on Dugouts at A.D.S. began.	MuR
BAILLEUL	3.6.15		Weather bright and cool - Sunshine - Water Survey of district made by Bearers Continued by Lt. MacPherson R.A.M.C.	MuR MuR
BAILLEUL	4.6.15		Cold cloudy and dull - nothing unusual to report - Deadly A.D.M.S. lectures. Messing staff.	MuR MuR
BAILLEUL	5.6.15		Dull and cloudy - rain. Cold - nothing unusual to Report	AuR
BAILLEUL	6.6.16		Nothing unusual to report. No aerial activity	MuR
BAILLEUL	7.6.16		Weather still cool. Some Sunshine	AuR
BAILLEUL	8.6.16		Inspection of H.Q. Unit by G.O.C. 5th Corps - un A.D.M.S. 5 Corps	MuR
BAILLEUL	9.6.16		Weather still cold - nothing unusual to report	MuR
BAILLEUL	10.6.16		Weather still dull and cold - nothing unusual to report.	MuR
BAILLEUL	11.6.16		Weather bleak and cold.	MuR

WAR DIARY / INTELLIGENCE SUMMARY

Army Form C. 2118.

74th Field Ambulance

32

Place	Date	Hour	Summary of Events and Information	Remarks and references to Appendices
BAILLEUL	12.6.16		Weather still wet & chilly. Lethy unusual to report - our hut generally quiet - no one on duty - at ADS (ordinary duty) any kits made	[initials]
BAILLEUL	13.6.16		huts wet - cold - no heavy cases	[initials]
BAILLEUL	14.6.16		Weather still cold - Wx so wet - Lethy unusual to report - our details	[initials]
BAILLEUL	15.6.16		1 hut Bay Saint. Weather rather warmer - no rain -	[initials]
BAILLEUL	16.6.16		Weather brighter, sunshine, no rain. GAS ALERT.	[initials]
BAILLEUL	17.6.16		Weather improving. Gas attack last night. 23 cases passed thro' ADS – went to CCS – etc case late in morning – No gas at Reninghelst Collecting Post in NEUVE EGLISE Road – a certain	[initials]
BAILLEUL	18.6.16		amount of gas at DS. Romarin – Weather still rather cool – Visit ADS & DS. Collecting Post. – Visit from DDMS & Corps	[initials]
BAILLEUL	19.6.16		Weather still chilly – Visit Dressing Station why unusual to report.	[initials]
BAILLEUL	20.6.16		Weather during States – huts generally quiet.	[initials]

Army Form C. 2118.

WAR DIARY
or
INTELLIGENCE SUMMARY.

7th Field Ambulance

39

(Erase heading not required.)

Instructions regarding War Diaries and Intelligence Summaries are contained in F. S. Regs., Part II. and the Staff Manual respectively. Title pages will be prepared in manuscript.

Place	Date	Hour	Summary of Events and Information	Remarks and references to Appendices
BAILLEUL	21.6.16	—	Weather warm. Nothing unusual to report	Author Koch
BAILLEUL	22.6.16	—	Handed over Collecting Post on NEUVE EGLISE Road to 1st Australian Fd Amb. Units due out - interviews - Pro. of No. 1 A.F.A. 1st A.D.S.	Auth
BAILLEUL	23.6.16	—	Weather improving - nothing unusual to report	Auth
BAILLEUL	24.6.16	—	Weather better - Lunch Smith. Visits Divary Statn RomARIN	Auth
BAILLEUL	25.6.16	—	Visit Hd Qtrs 24 Division - weather warm - brilliant sunshine.	Auth
BAILLEUL	26.6.16	—	Weather dull - some rain - nothing unusual to report	Auth
BAILLEUL	27.6.16	—	Weather warm - some rain.	Auth
BAILLEUL	28.6.16	—	Visit to new billeting area at MONT. NOIR. - visit Divary Statn RomARIN	Auth
BAILLEUL	29.6.16	—	Visit to Billeting area at LOCRE. - visits Divary Statn RomARIN Farenye, handing over to No. 7 Australian Fd Ambulance - Motor Colly Ambulance on trucks during the night hourly in 27 wounded passing through on Divary Station	Auth

2353 Wt. W2544/1454 700,000 5/15 D. D. & L. A.D.S.S./Forms/C. 2118.

Army Form C. 2118.

WAR DIARY
or
INTELLIGENCE SUMMARY. 74 Field Ambulance.
(Erase heading not required.)

No. 40.

Instructions regarding War Diaries and Intelligence Summaries are contained in F. S. Regs., Part II. and the Staff Manual respectively. Title pages will be prepared in manuscript.

Place	Date	Hour	Summary of Events and Information	Remarks and references to Appendices
BAILLEUL	30.6.16		To new location at MONT NOIR to make arrangements for 120 sick. Located a temporary Div. Rest Station. Visited ADMS 24 Division. Further arrangements made.	Archive ltr cr.

Archive
War Diary
O.C. 74 Field Ambulance

Army Form C. 348.

MEMORANDUM.

From ADMS
      24th Divn

To DAG
     3rd Echelon

From

To

ANSWER.

_2-9-_ 1916.

_____ 191

Enclosed herewith is
War Diary for August
1916 — 24th Divl.
HQ. Medical Services.

[Stamp: ASSISTANT DIRECTOR MEDICAL SERVICES
No. M514
Date 2-9-16
24th DIVISION]

Tipsett
Capt DADMS
for Lieut. ADMS
     24 Divn.

24th Division

74th Field Ambulance

July 1916

H.Q. 24th Division

Attached please find original War Diaries for month of July, for favour of transmission to A.G's Office, Base. Kindly acknowledge receipt.

signature
Lieut Col R.A.M.C.
Officer Commdg. 74th Field Ambulance

WAR DIARY
INTELLIGENCE SUMMARY

Army Form C. 2118

74 Field Ambulance

Vol. 10

July 24

Place	Date	Hour	Summary of Events and Information	Remarks and references to Appendices
MONT NOIR	1.7.16		Handed over HQ at BAILLEUL to 7 Australian Field Ambulance at 2 pm - and others at new HQ Mont Noir at 3 pm - HQ on West side from Tent.	Mr. Rees Major
MONT NOIR	2.7.16		Morning. Helped to arrange table across trestle manager - Colonel and two walls in LOCRE area - weather behaved - heavy thunderstorm by British Guns S. of ARMENTIERES. -	Major
MONT NOIR	3.7.16		Weather warm - brilliant sunshine - Italic shelling in direction of ARANOUTRES. - Considerable enemy aerial activity. -	Major
MONT NOIR	4.7.16		Weather bad - heavy rain - Thunderstorm - Visit by Sen. Officer 2nd Army.	Major
MIDNT NOIR	5.7.16		B Section sent to METEREN to relieve Rest Station and 100 pounds casualties transferred there from 72 Field Ambulance - weather warm, thundery	Major
MONT NOIR	6.7.16		Weather damp and chill - troops from D.D.M.S. IX Corps -	Major
MONT NOIR	7.7.16		Weather warm and cloudy -	Major
MONT NOIR	8.7.16		C Section to METEREN - taken over Baths at LA BOSACE - N of METEREN.	Major
MONT NOIR	9.7.16		C Section to BAILLEUL from METEREN - Hotter rain also H.Q. hits and officer to become barracks	Major

Army Form C. 2118.

WAR DIARY
or
INTELLIGENCE SUMMARY.
74 Field Ambulance 42

(Erase heading not required.)

Instructions regarding War Diaries and Intelligence Summaries are contained in F. S. Regs., Part II. and the Staff Manual respectively. Title pages will be prepared in manuscript.

Place	Date	Hour	Summary of Events and Information	Remarks and references to Appendices
Mont Noir	10-7-16		Weather fine and windy – Considerable Enemy aerial activity during the night.	Air Recon Report
Mont Noir	11-7-16		Weather cold and cloudy – Went to A.D.M.S. 24 Division at Bailleul – Nothing unusual to report.	A.M.R.
Mont Noir	12-7-16		Dull and cloudy – cold –	A.M.R.
Mont Noir	13-7-16		Weather windy – Some rain –	A.M.R. Appdx
Mont Noir	14-7-16		Weather rather cold –	Appdx
Mont Noir	15-7-16		Weather clearing –	Intt
Mont Noir	16-7-16		To Bailleul to see A.D.M.S. – Having unusual amount of sickness, but no regards Enemy activity nothing unusual to report	A.M.R.
Mont Noir	17-7-16		To Bailleul to see A.D.M.S. – Nothing unusual to report	A.M.R.
Mont Noir	18-7-16		To Bailleul further evidence – Heavy due am. Some hostile shelling of Dranoutre. Cloudy –	A.M.R.
Mont Noir	19-7-16		Nothing unusual – Joe See A.D.M.S. – Report	A.M.R.
Mont Noir	20-7-16		Handed over B. sectn area at Berthen to 72 Field Ambulance & C sectn area in Bailleul to 61 Field Ambulance, – whole unit Ambulance encamped at Mont Noir.	Intt

Army Form C. 2118.

WAR DIARY
or
INTELLIGENCE SUMMARY.

74 Field Ambulance

43

(Erase heading not required.)

Instructions regarding War Diaries and Intelligence Summaries are contained in F. S. Regs, Part II. and the Staff Manual respectively. Title pages will be prepared in manuscript.

Place	Date	Hour	Summary of Events and Information	Remarks and references to Appendices
METEREN	22/7/16		Ambulance moves from MONT NOIR to METEREN. 1st class – Weather fine – Troops in huts.	Auth. Iter.
METEREN	23/7/16		Visit of Capt. J. McBrinley Gunn as Chief medical.	Nu. R.
METEREN	24/7/16		Leave Ambulance entrain at 7.08 pm. at BAILLEUL train station – Entrain in our huts – Train left at 10.28 pm. –	Nu. R.
CAVILLON (SOMME)	25/7/16		Train arrive LONGUEAU – 5 kilometres SW of AMIENS at 8 am – Ambulance breakfasts – fed travellers horses – ambulance via AMIENS – DREUIL – AILLY – BREILLY – FOUDRINOY – to CAVILLON, arriving 6.30 pm. – Officers in billets – men huts in town – Weather warm and close – Then marches well – Hôtel duties in kermotis. –	Nu. R.
CAVILLON	26/7/16		Weather fine – Men resting – Usually troops foot – visit for asking 24° down.	Nu. R.
CAVILLON	27/7/16		Weather fine – Nothing unusual to report – All men in unit have been inoculated with T.A.B.	Nu. R.
CAVILLON	28/7/16		Weather fine – nothing unusual to report.	Nu. R.

Army Form C. 2118.

WAR DIARY
or
INTELLIGENCE SUMMARY.
(Erase heading not required.)

74 b/t Ambulance 44

Place	Date	Hour	Summary of Events and Information	Remarks and references to Appendices
CAVILLON	29.7.16		Heavy rains - chow day - bathing - nothing unusual to report	Medical tract.
CAVILLON	30.7.16		Sanford left CAVILLON at 10:30 p.m. Evacuated 5 N.Z. Bearing Hospital AMIENS.	Aux.S.
CAVILLON	31.7.16		Left CAVILLON 7.30 am. Entrain diverted - failing that at PICQUIGNY. at 9.30 am. Detrained MÉRICOURT L'ABBÉ 2.30 pm. marched to huts near BUIRE CORPS dump) TREUX on to CORBIE-BRAY road S. Arriving 4.30 pm. At 7.30, 3 Officers, 6 N.C.O's and 108 other ranks rendezvous joined 17 INF Bde. at BOIS DE TAILLES taking over the Advanced Dressing Station. Ambulance began motor-cart equipment. Capt P.J. W.E. Donville Payne being them Ambulance to Service by the units of 17th Service Corps Cavalry to Start off to shift the field "dead."	M.R.

A. Rose
Major D. Name
O.C. 74 Field Ambulance

14th Field Ambulance.

2th to 10th

August 1916

COMMITTEE FOR THE MEDICAL HISTORY OF THE WAR
Date −9 OCT. 1916

Army Form C. 2118.

WAR DIARY
or
INTELLIGENCE SUMMARY.

7th Field Ambulance

(Erase heading not required.)

Place	Date	Hour	Summary of Events and Information	Remarks and references to Appendices
CORBIE (SOMME)	1.8.16		Appeared near DIVES CORPS. on CORBIE BRAY road at 9.20 a.m. — had observing of Tent Subdivision of 73rd and 7th Field Ambulances on transport plans units on march to CORBIE CHATEAU. on took over XIIIth Corps Rest Station there from 97 + 98 Field Ambulances — at 11.30 a.m. — B Rear Station at 1st S.W.O Pts. S/b of MEAULT. The Rest Station at CORBIE receives sick for XIIIth Corps — weather very warm as Sultry — brilliant sunshine.	A MR Rear Stat
CORBIE	2.8.16		Heavy Artillery group. 13 Corps. to transact duty — Lieut. Duncan + 8 others detailed to 45 CCS. VECQUEMONT for temporary duties — brilliant sunshine — nothing unusual to report. weather very warm.	Mr R
CORBIE	3.8.16		Located with 13 Corps — Lieut. & Wallis R.A.M.C. — Capt Duncan + 8 others	Mr R
CORBIE	4.8.16		Located with 13 Corps — nothing unusual to report — no unusual amount of sickness among the troops. — Heavy Gun fire last night.	Mr R
CORBIE	5.8.16		Nothing unusual to Report — train for Casons in division — Brilliant Sunshine.	Mr R
CORBIE	6.8.16		Rain Squall — Brilliant Sunshine — Visit from Lt. Col ADMS 13 Corps.	Mr R
CORBIE	7.8.16		Very little — No disease prevalent among troops — General health very good.	Mr R

Army Form C. 2118.

WAR DIARY
or
INTELLIGENCE SUMMARY.
(Erase heading not required.)

74 Field Ambulance 46

Instructions regarding War Diaries and Intelligence Summaries are contained in F. S. Regs., Part II. and the Staff Manual respectively. Title pages will be prepared in manuscript.

Place	Date	Hour	Summary of Events and Information	Remarks and references to Appendices
CORBIE	8.8.16	—	Bearer Division of 74th Field Ambulance moved up to A.D.S. at N end of BERNAFAY WOOD. Transport & Bearers moved on to HAPPY VALLEY. 62d N.E. L8c. —	H.McR.
CORBIE	9.8.16		Weather chill and cool. Slightly increased 15 report — at MERRYMAN — to 3rd C.C.S. — sick	J.McR.
CORBIE	10.8.16		Weather hot and cooler. — Nothing unusual to report	J.McL
CORBIE	11.8.16		Weather dry and warm — brilliant sunshine. Nothing unusual to report	J.McL
CORBIE	12.8.16		Nil — Admis to Division — Weather fine. —	J.McL
CORBIE	13.8.16		Sgt. Poulson — wounded by Shell and evacuated this No 5 C.C.S. — from BERNAFAY WOOD. Capt King and Capt Andrews return from visit Bearer Divisn — return for rest period to BRONFAY FARM — NE of BRAY.	J.McL
CORBIE	14.8.16		Weather damp. — Fine rain. — circular round of CORBIE. Presentation Officers and men admitted to Corps Rest Station.	J.McL
CORBIE	15.8.16		Nothing unusual to report. — Weather rather dull. — some rain. —	J.McR.
CORBIE	16.8.16		Weather still dull — some rain — Capt Andrews to Main Dressing Station at Sapper Cairn. NE of BRAY. for temporary duty. Visit hm to our 14 Corps.	J.McL
CORBIE	18.8.16		Capt King sent L-21 C.C.S. for temporary duty. Visit from A.D.M.S. 14 Corps. Weather fair — No rain —	J.McR.

Army Form C. 2118.

WAR DIARY
or
INTELLIGENCE SUMMARY. 74 Field Ambulance

(Erase heading not required.)

Instructions regarding War Diaries and Intelligence Summaries are contained in F. S. Regs., Part II. and the Staff Manual respectively. Title pages will be prepared in manuscript.

47

Place	Date	Hour	Summary of Events and Information	Remarks and references to Appendices
CORBIE	19.8.16		Rear Division in action – 47948 Pte GOFF. H. killed – admitted with bearers wounded – in region of TRONES WOOD. – GUILLEMONT.	Auth[or]ised Med.
CORBIE	20.8.16		Nothing unusual to report at XIV Corps Rest Station. – Bearers return prevalent.	Mu R.
CORBIE	21.8.16		Capt McCurrick reports that a draft left was attd. by enemy shell fire in the evacuating dug out occupied by men of 74th Fd. Amb. near BERNAFAY WOOD at 9 am & 2½ pm Casualties. L/Cpl T.E BULMER. au 65251 Pte W.A DUNSTONE. killed	Mu R.
CORBIE	22.8.16		Bearer Division came out of the line this evening. to camp in HAPPY VALLEY. Enemy reaching Corbie – no rain – Bearers still prevalent among troops	Mu R.
CORBIE	23.8.16		Nothing unusual to report – Weather cooler –	Mu R. Mu R.
CORBIE	24.8.16		Pte Samuel Rawl. Bearer Divin. accidentally drowned – in MEAULT. – Nothing unusual to report. – Bearers among troops less prevalent.	Mu R.
CORBIE	25.8.16		Nothing unusual to report – Preparing to hand over to incoming unit –	Mu R.
CORBIE	26.8.16		Handed over BEF.7 Blocks. XIV Corps Rest Station to 14 Field Ambulance at 8 am – Marched off at 9.15 am via MERICOURT – L'ABBÉ – au TREUX – to BUIRE –	Mu R.
BUIRE – SUR – L'ANCRE.	27.8.16		arriving 12.30 noon – Rain storms at intervals. – Bivouacs in field – Bearer Division infirmaries units –	Auth

Army Form C. 2118.

WAR DIARY
or
INTELLIGENCE SUMMARY.

(Erase heading not required.)

74 Field Ambulance   No. 48

Place	Date	Hour	Summary of Events and Information	Remarks and references to Appendices
BUIRE Sur L'ANCRE	28/5/16	—	Visit from A.D.M.S. 24 Division - Handed to 42 Field Ambulance to hotels camp will move to taking over - site of camp 1/2 mile S.E. of ALBERT. - Sent advance party to looking of 1 mile to ADMS.	McRae A.D.S. Rear Rare
BUIRE	29/5/16		Heavy rain and thunderstorm.	Mil R.
ALBERT	30/5/16		Left BUIRE at 10.30 am - heavy rain - bad tracks via BERNAFAY - to hit 1/2 mile from ALBERT on (E)ALBERT - BRICOURT road - took over from 42 FIELD AMB. - and established DIVISIONAL REST CAMP. - Visited 19th FIELD AMBULANCES. Met men to taking over camp near BÉCORDEL. - Rained heavily all day.	An R.
ALBERT	31/5/16		Took over camp at BÉCORDEL from 19th Field Ambulance - 1 Sgt. 2 Cpls and 36 bearers Lent to 74 Field Ambulance. Accident in Bearer Subdivision Impeded - Sgt. Steven F. and 3 men wounded by shell bursting in Bomers - Part stolen his tent.	MuR

An Rae
McIvacone
O.C. 74 Field Ambulance.

140/1134

24.1.10.

7th Field Ambulance.

COMMITTEE FOR THE
MEDICAL HISTORY OF T.... W/...
Date 30 OCT. 1916

Army Form C. 2118.

74 Field Ambulance 49

WAR DIARY
or
INTELLIGENCE SUMMARY.

(Erase heading not required.)

Instructions regarding War Diaries and Intelligence Summaries are contained in F. S. Regs., Part II. and the Staff Manual respectively. Title pages will be prepared in manuscript.

Place	Date	Hour	Summary of Events and Information	Remarks and references to Appendices
ALBERT.	1/9/16	—	Handed over Dressing Station at BECOURT to 2/1 W. Lancs. Field Ambulance. — Lts. Ranford and Bruges round to 72nd Field Ambulance. — Association Evacuation of wounded. — Res. C/R Red C3. to No Corps Rest Station. (Pyrenees NYD) — — 515740. Cpl. Green on round. Wounded by shell fire and evacuated. —	The Rue
ALBERT.	2/9/16		Pte. Atkinson reported wounded – hysterical – healthy facing wound – Capt. Curries & Capt. H? Currie with 40 bearers left at 6 a.m. to report to O.C. 72nd Field Amb. at NAMETZ for duty. — Visit from ADSMS by Bernin. — Capt. Duncan to E.C.S. (Pyrenees NYD)	Anvil R
ALBERT.	3/9/16		Horse lines shelled at 10 a.m. by Germans – horse horses – no casualties. Animals wound Nat 53413 Pte. Meade A. was killed by shell fire on 1st Sept and Pte. Bowser, stretcher bearer wounded by shell fire. – Evening 7.30 Right tail was considerable amount of shelling between of own lines by the Germans. —	Anvil R
ALBERT.	4/9/16		Nothing unusual to report. — —	Anvil
BUIRE.	5/9/16		Handed over camp to 3/2 W.Lancs Field Amb. 55 Div. and left camp at 3 p.m. Route via MEAULT and DERNAN COURT to BUIRE. arriving 5 p.m. – bivouacs in field. – health good.	Anvil R

Army Form C. 2118.

WAR DIARY
or
INTELLIGENCE SUMMARY. 74 Field Ambulance

(Erase heading not required.)

Instructions regarding War Diaries and Intelligence Summaries are contained in F. S. Regs., Part II. and the Staff Manual respectively. Title pages will be prepared in manuscript.

No. 50.

Place	Date	Hour	Summary of Events and Information	Remarks and references to Appendices
BUIRE.	6/9/16	—	Horse transport left at 9 am under Capt McCurrick — Route - HEILLY - BONNAY - CORBIE - VECQUEMONT - AMIENS - ARGOEUVES — when billets for night — Rest of Transport left at 10 am - Dismounts following with ambulances at EDGEHILL - BERNANCOURT at 2 p.m. — Sick & wounded cases of — transferred to 21 Field Amb. of - BUIRE before departure	Special Itat
ERGNIES.	7/9/16	—	Dismounts portion of unit detrained at 10 pm 6/9/16 at LONGPRÉ - and marched via L'ETOILE - AILLY - to ERGNIES - arriving 2 a.m. 7/9/16 - were billeted - Transport left ARGOEUVES route via LA CHAUSSÉE - TIRANCOURT - FLIXECOURT - arriving ERGNIES at 4.30 p.m. - Hectic been on duty — Unit engaged in general fatigue work — hedging & cleaning etc - Very little churches - their beams in inches	Mu R.
ERGNIES.	8/9/16		Hectic fris - nothing unusual to report - Fine weather, hardening rapidly & inches	Mu R.
ERGNIES.	9/9/16			Mu R.
ERGNIES.	10/9/16		Visit from ADMS 24 Division - Health fair on Coal.	Mu R.

Army Form C. 2118.

WAR DIARY
or
INTELLIGENCE SUMMARY.
(Erase heading not required.)

74 Field Ambulance 51.

Place	Date	Hour	Summary of Events and Information	Remarks and references to Appendices
ERQUINES	11.9.16		Weather fine - 7154 C/Cpl SIMMONDS T. R.A.M.C has been awarded the Conduct Medal for gallantry in action on Aug 18th	MuR MacMahon
ERQUINES	12.9.16		Visit from Major Gen. J. Capper CB. G.O.C. 24 Division - He went round to 3rd Brigade for tea but lunched here in the Division - owing to epidemic from all units in the Division - Weather fine - Shoals of troops going - very few cases of diarrhoea	MuR
ERQUINES	13.9.16		Inspection of Camp by G.O.C. 24th Division -- Weather rather dull some rain	MuR
ERQUINES	14.9.16		Arrival of 15th reinforcements from ROUEN - Weather cooler - few fresh ambulance	MuR
ERQUINES	15.9.16		1 Officer + 50 other ranks proceed today to two day's visit to seaside Camp at AULT. - Nothing unusual to report	MuR MuR
ERQUINES	16.9.16		Weather - Good - Nothing unusual to Report	MuR
ERQUINES	17.9.16		Weather hot - heavy rain - Nothing unusual to report	MuR
ERQUINES	18.9.16		Weather wet - Nothing unusual to report	MuR

Army Form C. 2118.

WAR DIARY
or
INTELLIGENCE SUMMARY.

(Erase heading not required.)

74th Field Ambulance. S2

Place	Date	Hour	Summary of Events and Information	Remarks and references to Appendices
ERGNIES	19.9.16		Left ERGNIES at 4 pm. route via AILLY to PONT REMY - Fresh Ambulance entraines and left at 8pm - weather fine - Detachment on leave of absence	Ambulance Steel
PRESSY	20.9.16		Regnier at PONT REMY on 7.15 pm. as entraines also - Arrived PERNES station at 3 a.m., detraines and marches to PRESSY arriving at 4.30 a.m. kept rate high - weather damp some rain - Motor Transport fm 30 Division arrived - minus 2 motor cycles	Amb.
PRESSY	21.9.16		Nothing unusual to report - weather fine - no prevailing disease - Capt King Ranc sent to ESTREE to inspect new Fresh Ambulance location - Also to CAVCOURT to install ARS	Amb.
PRESSY	22.9.16		Went to ESTREE to arrange details of taking over dressing station and ARS at CAVCOURT and laundry at HOUDAIN fm S.African Fresh Ambulance	Amb
HOUDAIN	23.9.16		Left PRESSY at 3 pm and marched via PERNES - Divion to HOUDAIN arriving at 5 pm - Went into Huts here - Took over laundry there fm S.A. Fresh Amb	Amb
HOUDAIN	24.9.16		Left HOUDAIN at 7 a.m. arrives ESTREE at 9 a.m. took over a holding dressing station took over ARS at CAVCOURT fm S.African Fresh Ambulance and Czechs took over ARS at CAVCOURT fm S.African Fresh Ambulance	Amb

WAR DIARY
INTELLIGENCE SUMMARY

Army Form C. 2118.

74 Field Ambulance   53

Place	Date	Hour	Summary of Events and Information	Remarks and references to Appendices
ESTRÉE CAUCHIE	25/9/16		Arrival of Dressing Station at ESTRÉE - Brig. at CAUCOURT aux Bureau Sanitary at HOUDAIN au Fort Hôtel & improvements about hospital billets at VILLERS-AU-BOIS.	AmRene Lieut.
ESTRÉE	26/9/16		Little going on - no prisoners coming through - nothing much to report	Mul
ESTRÉE	27/9/16		Lecture given. Used five MTMS 24th Division the class meets D.R.S. at CAUCOURT town for lecture by SOC in Div.	Mul
ESTRÉE	28/9/16		Visited by DDMS M. Corps.	Mul
ESTRÉE	29/9/16		Nothing unusual to report - the Infantry divisions - are advancing	Mul
ESTRÉE	30/9/16		At Dressing Station, D.R.S. - Sanitary authorities	Mul

AmRene
Lieut Renie
O.C. 74 Field Ambulance

140/87

24th Div.

74th Field Ambulance.

Oct. 1916

COMMITTEE FOR THE
MEDICAL HISTORY OF THE WAR
Date 9 DEC. 1916

Army Form C. 2118.

WAR DIARY
or
INTELLIGENCE SUMMARY
(Erase heading not required.)

74 Field Ambulance   No. 54

Place	Date	Hour	Summary of Events and Information	Remarks and references to Appendices
ESTREE-CAUCHY	1/10/16		Inspecting Laundry at HOUDAIN and baths at VILLARS-AU-BOIS and at GOUY-SERVIN. - Weather good - chilly - very few flies. Inspected 8th Norfolk Iron Recon etc. - Inspected Baths at VILLERS at Capt. H.C. Wright. Rains later in strength - weather wet -	AMR en Charge MR
ESTREE	2/10/16		Inspected Ruthwood and Harris Camp. Lt. Harris rejoin 107th Bde R.F.A. - Locatelli left went to join 37th Divn as Assistant vet. will Evening Lakeley still at Villars-au-Gouy.	MR
ESTREE	3/10/16		Weather wet. Instructional dressing - visits D.A.D.S - Laundry - Baths at Villars - Free BATHING ie - Anglin supply & Clothing Laundry. Hawes and Connant to Capt SR. Savoye herewo duty. Major Renic before quit in leave	MR
ESTREE	4/10/16		Lt. Col. A.M. Rose proceeded on leave + took over command of the 4 And. Inspection of camp & personnel. Weather fine, wind very high. Ear Abbot Th. Hon RA + Q.M W.J.C. Merryman proceeds on leave today	MR
ESTREE	5/10/16			MK

Place	Date	Hour	Summary of Events and Information	Remarks and references to Appendices
ESTREE	VI-10-16		Weather wet. Difficulty in finding sufficient men to carry on the work on the Ambulance so split up into four sections. Invariably engaged. Today 1 NCO 11 O.R. proceeded to Aubigny to break flag for roadside. Rations requisitioned by IVth Corps.	DMM
ESTREE	VII-10/16		Capt. J.V.O. Andrews R.A.M.C. was today transferred to 37th Division, by order of A.D.M.S. 24th Division, via strength of the unit from 8-10-16. Capt. W.F. McDonald R.A.M.C. proceeded to Caucourt to take over command of the D.R.S. vice Capt. J.V.O. Andrews to 37th Div. Very short of officers & men. Today, 5 Privates of the R.A.M.C. proceeded to NIEPPE FOREST to cut wood, under the command of the IVth Corps. Today we cut down the staff of the officers mess hospital, in order to procure enough men to carry on the work round the grounds &c. No fag was available today, very little work was done on the camp roads.	DMM
ESTREE	VIII-10/16		Camp inspected today by Brigadier Genl. Carroll of the 13th Inf. Brigade. Report good. Heavy rain. Great deal of indoor work done.	DMM

Army Form C. 2118.
56.

WAR DIARY
or
INTELLIGENCE SUMMARY
(Erase heading not required.)

Place	Date	Hour	Summary of Events and Information	Remarks and references to Appendices
ESTREE	9.10.16		Inspected CAUCOURT today, work progressing steadily but slowly. Made arrangements with C.R.E. to obtain acetylene on account of the shortage of personnel. Latrines at VILLARS AU BOIS very insanitary. Bathing arrangements good. CAPT. P.J. (A.I.R.A.M.C. reported his arrival for duty today re lecture the strength from 8-10-16. Vice Capt J.V.O Andrews (R.M.C. (auth A.D.M.S 24th Div). Parade inspection of Iron Rations, Q as helmets & clothing & personnel today 2 p.m. Concert for patients & personnel at night off-	JMcK
ESTREE	10.10/16		O.H.P.T. McGuirk proceeded up to the trenches today on temporary duty with the 20 R. Brig. Great deal of work done today both at C.A.O.COURT. Where three are now our Sappers & two men of a Labour Battalion attached no slag obtainable again, work greatly hindered.	JMcK
ESTREE	11.10/16		Inspected Laundry at Houdain today, also Baths at VILLARS AU BOIS both working well. Suggested that the Laundry should be lit by Electric light which is very cheap.	JMcK

Army Form C. 2118.
57

WAR DIARY
or
INTELLIGENCE SUMMARY
(Erase heading not required.)

Place	Date	Hour	Summary of Events and Information	Remarks and references to Appendices
ESTRÉES	12/10		Inspected CAUCOURT today. Holiday practically at a standstill on the Roads in Camp. D.D.M.S. Corps inspected CAUCOURT in afternoon. Expressed himself satisfied as to the work being done. Thick disinfector at Laundry giving a great of trouble - not efficient.	DMM
	13.10.16		Report received today that "B" Section treatment was in very bad condition, strung out who cared as to cleaning, cart thoroughly scrubbed out with boiling water & a strong sol of Chloride of lime. Both proceeding rapidly well, weather bad, cold raw.	DMM
	14.10.16		Inspected VILLARS AU BOIS & CAUCOURT; working excellent, all looks in good order. Purative disease seems to spread, probably due to the prevailing bad weather. C.R.E. agreed to make Cpt Gillis to us to the design of our 41st Sanitary Section. Pte Brown brigade message reported back in duty today. Green envelopes issued to the Division again.	DMM

WAR DIARY
or
INTELLIGENCE SUMMARY
(Erase heading not required.)

Army Form C. 2118.

Place	Date	Hour	Summary of Events and Information	Remarks and references to Appendices
ESTREE	15/10/16		Divine Service for all troops in hospital, weather greatly improved & much progress made with the camp roads, latrine, cook the D.R.S. Inspection of D.R.S. in afternoon, progress rapid work excellent in quality.	DDMS
ESTREE	16/10/16		Lt. Col. A.M. ROSE RAMC & hon Lt & Q.M. W.S.C. MERRIMAN returned from leave. Lt. Col. A.M Rose proceeded to Divisional H.Q. to act as A.D.M.S. during the absence of Col. Buswell RAMC on leave. S. Sgt Major J. RILEY A.S.C. ho I/c 210393, was attached to the F. Ambulance for duty. A/Sgt WEBSTER R. to Cpl. S.-Sick. Weather improving. Frost in morning. Roadwork proceeding rapidly. Camp improving greatly.	DDMS
ESTREE	17/10/16		CAPT. W.F. McDONALD reported sick today. Plentiful supply of water was of tapwater today for the first time from the large water tanks erected back the shelter from the Rhone Filters length of the patients huts — four of the same	DDMS

2449 Wt. W14957/M90 750,000 1/16 J.B.C. & A. Forms/C.2118/12.

Army Form C. 2118.

WAR DIARY
or
INTELLIGENCE SUMMARY
(Erase heading not required.)

59.

Place	Date	Hour	Summary of Events and Information	Remarks and references to Appendices
ESTREE	19/4/6		CAPT. W.F. MacDONALD R.A.M.C. was evacuated to CCS today. CAPT. J.P. CAHIR. R.A.M.C. took over command of the D.R.S. at CAUCOURT Bay, vice CAPT. W.F. MacDONALD R.A.M.C. to C.C.S. A/Cpl. 2154 SIMMONDS.T. to be A/sgt with pay (Authority DDMS 14th Corps. 24/34 d/18-10-16.) 39,071. S.Sgt. ROBERTS. I.M. to be Q.M.S. (Authority. Corps Routine orders. R.A.M.C. No 37 d/4-10-16.) 37,591. Sgt. SIMPSON.A.R. to be Staff Sgt. (Authority Corps Routine orders. R.A.M.C. No 37. d/1(?)/10/16.) Very short of officers, only three medical officers actually serving with the unit, one at H.Q.F.A. one at D.R.S. 4. One at Laund M.	JPC

Place	Date	Hour	Summary of Events and Information	Remarks and references to Appendices
ESTREE	19/6/16		Plentiful supply of clay now obtainable & the road work is progressing rapidly. Inspection of the D.R.S. by Lt Col A.M. ROSE R.A.M.C. acting A.D.M.S., also of Laundry at HOUDAIN. Lack of timber is no return ing the building of structures at the D.R.S. but sans [sawn?] are being erected & more rapid progress is hoped for in the future.	A.D.M.S.
ESTREE	20/6/16		Rain fell heavily all day & work was chiefly of an indoor nature. A curious condition of the skin of the hands & feet of a patient admitted to the 62 Amb. was noticed today. It was akin to Scleroderma & yet was also like a deep rooted "ichthiosaurosis". It seemed to be due to immersion in mud. The skin was swollen, very hard & the	

Place	Date	Hour	Summary of Events and Information	Remarks and references to Appendices
ESTRÉE	20/10		Abrasions were perfectly straight but very deep & very painful. Scraped the parts with oil & oily substances so that the pain lessened somewhat.	JMR
ESTRÉE	21/10		Very frosty weather, clean, bright, sunshining day, but very cold. Gralled progress was made today. LT. COL. A.M. ROSE. R.A.M.C. & LT. & Q.M. W.J.C. MERRIMAN R.A.M.C. provided trews the area at present occupied by the 40th Div. in order to inspect the various working centres. CAPT. McCURRIE. R.A.M.C. returns today from the 3rd R.B. where he has been doing temporary duty.	JMR

Army Form C. 2118.

WAR DIARY
or
INTELLIGENCE SUMMARY

(Erase heading not required.)

62

Place	Date	Hour	Summary of Events and Information	Remarks and references to Appendices
ESTREE	22/10/16		Divine Service arrival. Report forwarded today from the Division, warning us that one of the Bandsmen - 8674 Pte Bishop's 2nd Casualties attached 14th F.Amb - Showed us executed rick is a suspicion of one of the Enteric group. In the London Gazette dated 11/10/16. — No. 515540. Cpl FREEMAN J.H. R.A.M.C. No. 49292. Pte. (A/Cpl) HAWKES J.H. R.A.M.C. awarded the MILITARY MEDAL. (Authority) D.R.O. 24th Div. dated 19/10/16 & 21/10/16.) Weather cold & sunshiny. Football match played today between the 7 F.Amb & the Divisional Train.	JPN/10

WAR DIARY

Army Form C. 2118.

63

Place	Date	Hour	Summary of Events and Information	Remarks and references to Appendices
ESTREE	23/10		Weather fine but cold. Inspection/previous carried out by officer. Pay as usual. Inspection of Gas Helmets & Iron rations & symptoms of personnel 10 a.m. 2 p.m. parade.	D.A.M.G.
ESTREE	24/10		Weather wet. Inspection of personnel. Gas no treated in expectation of an early burst. Canadian Division (1st) marching through the village anything unusual. All extra blankets were disinfected (pale) heather very cold + rain.	X.R.K

Army Form C. 2118.

WAR DIARY
or
INTELLIGENCE SUMMARY
(Erase heading not required.)

Place	Date	Hour	Summary of Events and Information	Remarks and references to Appendices
ESTREE	25/10/16		Weather again wet. A.D.M.S. Returning from leave awaited Col. A.M. ROSE will return to Unit tomorrow. Inspected Laundry at HOUDAIN, work excellent, place very clean & everything was satisfactory. Great deal of indoor work done today & much time spent in cleaning up the camp & buildings. Section Equipment checked. Lieut. B.C. HARTLEY. R.A.M.C. joined this unit today & is taken on the strength from this date. 25/10/16.	JMR JMR

Army Form C. 2118.

WAR DIARY
or
INTELLIGENCE SUMMARY
(Erase heading not required.)

74 Field Ambulance

Place	Date	Hour	Summary of Events and Information	Remarks and references to Appendices
ESTREE CAUCHES	26/10/16		Resumed Command of Unit on return of A.D.M.S. from leave - Supervise loading over Dressing Station Outfits - Kit lists lost - Inspector of Dressing Station Dinimere Rest Station, CAUCOURT - Sadly. HOUDAIN and Dinimere Rest Station.	Mr Roe Lt-Col
ESTREES CAUCHES	27/10/16		Capt. KING. D.R. - 2 N.C.O. and 20 O.R. left to join 73 Fd Ambulance for temporary duty. - 1 N.C.O. and 18 O.R. - 15 I Corps Rest Station AIRE - Advance Party from 3rd Canadian Field Ambulance arrived - D.R.S. CAUCOURT handed over.	Ami R.
LABEUVRIERE	28/10/16		Handed over Dressing Station at ESTREES to 3rd Canadian Fd Ambulance - Unit marched off at 10 am route via GAUCHIN - LS Gal - HOUDAIN - BRUAY - LAPUGNOY to LABEUVRIERE arriving there at 3.30 pm - took over from 157 Field Ambulance - in MONASTERY Rue - Caufous. 1st Corps Rest Station (A Section) - also Corps Officers Rest Station AIRE	Ami R.
LABEUVRIERE	29/10/16		Inspected Coys and Unit - took over charge of German Prisoners Camp at CROQUES - in addition to other work also - provide Town Major - for LABEUVRIERES - Supervision of Centenues, Disinfection of Cookhouse Commenced -	Ami R.
LABEUVRIERE	30/10/16		Inspected Coys and Unit - Nothing unusual to report - All in pounds Ambulance	Ami R.

Army Form C. 2118.

66

74 Field Ambulance

WAR DIARY
or
INTELLIGENCE SUMMARY

(Erase heading not required.)

Place	Date	Hour	Summary of Events and Information	Remarks and references to Appendices
LABEUVRIERE	31.10.16		Weather rather bright - rain at intervals - All movements on routine - Nothing unusual to report.	A. McRae Lt.Col.

A. McRae
Lt. Colonel
O.C. 74 Field Ambulance

140/862

24th Div.

14th Field Ambulance

COMMITTEE FOR THE
MEDICAL HISTORY OF THE WAR
Date −3 JAN. 1917

aargm4
24 Division

Secret

Attached please find original War Diaries for month of November 1916. Kindly acknowledge receipt.

A.M.Rose

Lieut Col R.A.M.C.
Officer Commdg. 74th Field Ambulance

Army Form C. 2118.

WAR DIARY
or
INTELLIGENCE SUMMARY
(Erase heading not required.)

114 Field Ambulance
R.A.M.C.

Instructions regarding War Diaries and Intelligence Summaries are contained in F. S. Regs., Part II. and the Staff Manual respectively. Title Pages will be prepared in manuscript.

Place	Date	Hour	Summary of Events and Information	Remarks and references to Appendices
LABEUVRIERE	1/11/16		Weather Good. Inspection of 1st Corps Rest Station (A. Section) with Chief Engineer 1st Corps regarding proposed new Cookhouse. Evening Rooms and new latrines and washhouse for B. Block. Visit from DADMS 24th Division.	Am. R.A. & ADMS Memo
LABEUVRIERE	2/11/16		Inspection of 1st Corps Rest Station by DDMS 1st Corps and ADMS 24th Division. All improvements continued.	Am. R.
LABEUVRIERE	3/11/16		Patients in Hospice paid. All improvements continued. Weather fair.	Shr. R.
LABEUVRIERE	4/11/16		Gas Drill (personnel). Visits 1st Corps Officers Rest Station AIRE. Weather fine, hot-cold - occasional showers.	Mr. R.
LABEUVRIERE	5/11/16		Visit of inspection by DDMS 1st Corps - Service service 2 pm - Inn's high - Sunshine - Heads of hospo good. No hindering disease.	Mr. R.
LABEUVRIERE	6/11/16		Weather bad - whig - finance to report.	Shr. L.
LABEUVRIERE	7/11/16		Weather still bad - heavy rain. All improvements continued.	Shr. L.
LABEUVRIERE	8/11/16		Weather wet - visits General Province Camp at CHOCQUES - am 1st Corps Officers Rest Station AIRE. Weather less - heavy rain.	Mr. L.

Army Form C. 2118.
68

WAR DIARY
or
INTELLIGENCE SUMMARY

(Erase heading not required.)

74 Field Ambulance

Instructions regarding War Diaries and Intelligence Summaries are contained in F. S. Regs., Part II. and the Staff Manual respectively. Title Pages will be prepared in manuscript.

Place	Date	Hour	Summary of Events and Information	Remarks and references to Appendices
ABEUVRIERE	9/11/16	—	Inspection of Corps Rest Station by G.O.C. 21 Division and A.D.M.S. — Weather fine, brilliant sunshine. — Lt. HARTLEY RANC. left for Ineford Surg. with 12 Royal Fusiliers.	Am Rem Lt Col
ABEUVRIERE	10/11/16		Weather good — nothing unusual to report.	Am R.
LABEUVRIERE	11/11/16		All in progress to continues — new latrines and urinals finished — Swan Row many completion — Poilus attention benches also commenced.	Ind.
LABEUVRIERE	12/11/16		Nothing unusual to report. — Visits from Rest Stations ARPS.	Am R.
LABEUVRIERE	13/11/16		All improvements continues — Centery sleep dear for road making — weather fine — no rain —	Am R.
LABEUVRIERE	14/11/16		Weather fine — Health of troops good.	Am R.
LABEUVRIERE	15/11/16		Weather fine and cold — All work progressing.	Am R.

Army Form C. 2118.

WAR DIARY
or
INTELLIGENCE SUMMARY

(Erase heading not required.)

74 Field Ambulance   69

Place	Date	Hour	Summary of Events and Information	Remarks and references to Appendices
LABEUVRIERE	16/11/16		Inspection of A. Section by C.O.C. 1st Corps Rest Station by A.D.M.S. 1st Corps.	Maybe kneel.
LABEUVRIERE	17/11/16		Weather very cold — seven frost — brilliant sunshine — All improvements being continued.	Mh R.
LABEUVRIERE	18/11/16		Nothing unusual to report — Steaming troops feet.	Mh R.
LABEUVRIERE	19/11/16		All work continues — Roadmaking — Hutching progressing.	Mhl
LABEUVRIERE	20/11/16		Weather cold. One rain. — Works - Bath Douanes School.	Mhl
LABEUVRIERE	21/11/16		Weather cold and damp — Nothing unusual to report.	Mhl
LABEUVRIERE	22/11/16		AIRE. It worked 1st Corps Officers Rest Station.	Mhl

Army Form C. 2118.

70

WAR DIARY
or
INTELLIGENCE SUMMARY

74 Field Ambulance

(Erase heading not required.)

Instructions regarding War Diaries and Intelligence Summaries are contained in F. S. Regs., Part II. and the Staff Manual respectively. Title Pages will be prepared in manuscript.

Place	Date	Hour	Summary of Events and Information	Remarks and references to Appendices
LABEUVRIERE	23/11/16	—	All work progressing in satisfactory manner. Weather cold - no rain.	Mr Rice Lieutenant Mr R
LABEUVRIERE	24/11/16	—	Nothing unusual to report - weather fair.	Mr R.
LABEUVRIERE	25/11/16	—	Influenza rather prevalent among patients and Ramc personnel. Weather wet and milder.	Mr R.
LABEUVRIERE	26/11/16	—	No rain - nothing unusual to report - new stretcher cases.	Mr R.
LABEUVRIERE	27/11/16	—	Weather cold - no rain - all improvements continued - during run completed - new kitchen oven completed.	Mr R.
LABEUVRIERE	28/11/16	—	Nothing unusual to report. - Cases of influenza few in number.	Mr R.
LABEUVRIERE	29/11/16	—	Weather very cold and damp. - new vaccination commenced - anthelmintic tablets in Sac Chamber -	Mr R.
LABEUVRIERE	30/11/16	—	Weather cold - no particularly disease	Mr R.

Arthur
Lieutenant
O.C. 74 Field Ambulance

14/1/03

24th Q23

14th Field Ambulance.

Dec 1916

COMMITTEE FOR THE
MEDICAL HISTORY OF THE W.
Date 31 JAN. 1917

T33L   74

Army Form C. 2118.

WAR DIARY
or
INTELLIGENCE SUMMARY

No. 74 Field Ambulance

Vol 15

(Erase heading not required.)

Place	Date	Hour	Summary of Events and Information	Remarks and references to Appendices
LABEUVRIERE	1/12/16		Weather cold and dampy - nothing unusual to report	Sunrise 7 cloudness MuL
LABEUVRIERE	2/12/16		Weather very cold - Several cases of Influenza among Rank & Personnel	MuL
LABEUVRIERE	3/12/16		Visit to 1st Corps Officers Rest Station, AIRE. -	MuL
LABEUVRIERE	4/12/16		Nothing unusual to report - Weather cold -	MuR
LABEUVRIERE	5/12/16		Inspection of 1st Corps Rest Station and 1st Corps Officers Rest Station by A.D.M.S. 24 Division	MuR
LABEUVRIERE	6/12/16		Visit to 1st Corps Officers Rest Station - Weather cold - Influenza still prevalent.	MuR
LABEUVRIERE	7/12/16		Inspection of 1st Corps Rest Station (RSC) by Major General Coffin CB. GOC 24 Division	MuL
LABEUVRIERE	8/12/16		Weather hot and cold - Cases of Influenza still prevalent.	MuL
LABEUVRIERE	9/12/16		Our impediments being cultivated - nothing unusual to report.	MuL
LABEUVRIERE	10/12/16		Weather still cold and wet -	SunR

Army Form C. 2118.

WAR DIARY
or
INTELLIGENCE SUMMARY

74 Field Ambulance

(Erase heading not required.)

Instructions regarding War Diaries and Intelligence Summaries are contained in F. S. Regs., Part II. and the Staff Manual respectively. Title Pages will be prepared in manuscript.

Place	Date	Hour	Summary of Events and Information	Remarks and references to Appendices
LABEUVRIÈRE	11/12/16	—	Nothing unusual to report - A few cases of influenza still occurring.	Andre Shortand
LABEUVRIÈRE	12/12/16	—	Some asking at Divnl. Intelligence to P.B. men -	Sh.R.
LABEUVRIÈRE	13/12/16		Weather cold and wet - nothing unusual to report -	Sh.R.
LABEUVRIÈRE	14/12/16		All work progressing satisfactorily - new stables almost complete, and hut unnel suspensis nearing completion.	Sh.R.
LABEUVRIÈRE	15/12/16		Nothing unusual to report - weather cold - but no much rain.	Sh.R.
LABEUVRIÈRE	16/12/16		Cases of Pyrexia N.Y.D. admitted to 1st C.R.S. Still large no. mules -	Sh.R.
LABEUVRIÈRE	17/12/16		Weather cold - Divine Service 2:30 pm. -	Sh.R.
LABEUVRIÈRE	18/12/16		Weather cold - no rain - nothing unusual to report	Sh.R.

2449 Wt. W14957/M90 750,000 1/16 J.B.C. & A. Forms/C.2118/12.

WAR DIARY
or
INTELLIGENCE SUMMARY

74 Field Ambulance

Army Form C. 2118.

Place	Date	Hour	Summary of Events and Information	Remarks and references to Appendices
LABEUVRIERE	19/12/16		Visit from Adml to Division. Weather cases. All references cases.	MtRue Lt Col
LABEUVRIERE	20/12/16		Mens to Freu au Bois Evacuation cupists.	
			A few cases of Influenza still occurring. Evacuation cupists. Weather cold and frosty.	JMuR.
LABEUVRIERE	21/12/16		Weather cold and wet. Nothing unusual to report	JMuR.
LABEUVRIERE	22/12/16		Wind high. Some rain. Influenza still prevalent.	JMuR.
LABEUVRIERE	23/12/16		Weather fine. Few cases. Nothing unusual to report.	JMuR.
LABEUVRIERE	24/12/16		Nothing unusual to report.	JMuR.
LABEUVRIERE	25/12/16		Xmas day. Weather wet.	JMuR.

Army Form C. 2118.

74.

WAR DIARY
or
INTELLIGENCE SUMMARY
(Erase heading not required.)

Instructions regarding War Diaries and Intelligence Summaries are contained in F. S. Regs., Part II and the Staff Manual respectively. Title Pages will be prepared in manuscript.

Place	Date	Hour	Summary of Events and Information	Remarks and references to Appendices
LABEUVRIERE	26/12/16	—	Pres. Stables inspected by Genl Surveys of Cavois — am reading made. Weather colder.	McRae Her
LABEUVRIERE	27/12/16	—	Weather dry and cold — Cases of Influenza less in number — Visit by a OMS 2nd Division —	JMcR
LABEUVRIERE	28/12/16	—	Nothing unusual to report — Some frost —	JMcR
LABEUVRIERE	29/12/16	—	Weather windy — no cases of Influenza among personal of unit.	JMcR.
LABEUVRIERE	30/12/16	—	Monthly Sanitary report sent to AOMS 2nd Division — Practice gas alarm at 5hm — Satisfactory	JMcR.
LABEUVRIERE	31/12/16	—	Weather rather mild — nothing unusual to report.	JMcR.

McRae
Lieut nanned
OC 74 Field Ambulance

114/1246

24th Nov.

14th Field Ambulance

COMMITTEE FOR THE
MEDICAL HISTORY OF THE WAR
Date 13 MAR. 1917

Army Form C. 2118.

WAR DIARY
or
INTELLIGENCE SUMMARY

74 Field Ambulance

VC/16

(Erase heading not required.)

Instructions regarding War Diaries and Intelligence Summaries are contained in F. S. Regs., Part II. and the Staff Manual respectively. Title Pages will be prepared in manuscript.

Place	Date	Hour	Summary of Events and Information	Remarks and references to Appendices
LABEUVRIERE	1.1.17		Weather very mild – Nothing unusual to report.	Mr Rae Sick
LABEUVRIERE	2/1/17		Weather still mild – Some rain – All work continues	Mult
LABEUVRIERE	3/1/17		Weather mild – wind high – Inspection of 1st Corps & their Rest Station by Corps 1st Corps.	Jm R.
LABEUVRIERE	4/1/17		Wet – Weather mild &c. – Nothing unusual to report	Jm R.
LABEUVRIERE	5/1/17		Nothing unusual to report –	Mult
LABEUVRIERE	6/1/17		Weather fair – rather mild – no prevalent disease –	Jm R.
LABEUVRIERE	7/1/17		Weather bracing – Snow Service 9 am –	Mult
LABEUVRIERE	8/1/17		Visit from G.O.C. 6th Division – Health Coes as heat.	

2449 Wt. W14957/Mg0 750,000 1/16 J.B.C. & A. Forms/C.2118/12.

WAR DIARY or INTELLIGENCE SUMMARY

74 Field Ambulance

Army Form C. 2118.
No. 76

Place	Date	Hour	Summary of Events and Information	Remarks and references to Appendices
LABEUVRIERE	9/1/17		Inspection of 1st Auxo Rest Station A Sec. by Brig. 1st Army – Btry & 1st Corps and ADMS 2d Division –	Mr R
LABEUVRIERE	10/1/17		Relieve Case & Directors Army Corps dues on return – French hurried other notified – C.O.W.S. 21st and 24th Division reinforced –	Mr R
LABEUVRIERE	11/1/17		Stragglers of 2nd Div case enquired – Stone pavers into y'rd –	Mr R
LABEUVRIERE	12/1/17		Weather cold and wet – nothing unusual to report – case transferred to C.R.S. area chiefly cases of "Pyrexia N.Y.D."	Mr R
LABEUVRIERE	13/1/17		Weather cold and wet – heavy rain – –	Mr R
LABEUVRIERE	14/1/17		Weather cold – and wet – nothing unusual to report	Mr R
LABEUVRIERE	15/1/17		Weather dull – no rain – nothing unusual to report.	Mr R

Army Form C. 2118.

WAR DIARY
or
INTELLIGENCE SUMMARY

(Erase heading not required.)

74 Field Ambulance   77.

Place	Date	Hour	Summary of Events and Information	Remarks and references to Appendices
LABEUVRIERE	16/1/17		Intense cold - some frost - One case of mumps to No 7 General Hospital	Duncan Weir
LABEUVRIERE	17/1/17		Intense cold - Snow - 2 inches during the night.	A.M.R.
LABEUVRIERE	18/1/17		Snow still lying - and falling at intervals - Nothing unusual to report.	A.M.R.
LABEUVRIERE	19/1/17		Frost - very cold at night - no Sickness prevalent.	A.M.R.
LABEUVRIERE	20/1/17		Visit to A.D.M.S. 24 Division - Health the CoS.	A.M.R.
LABEUVRIERE	21/1/17		Still cold - Frost at night - Intelligence Report.	A.M.R.
LABEUVRIERE	22/1/17		Very cold - No rain.	A.M.R.
LABEUVRIERE	23/1/17		Severe frost - Brilliant Sunshine - Nothing unusual to report.	A.M.R.

Army Form C. 2118.

WAR DIARY
or
INTELLIGENCE SUMMARY

(Erase heading not required.)

74 Field Ambulance

No. 78

Place	Date	Hour	Summary of Events and Information	Remarks and references to Appendices
LABEUVRIERE	24/7/17		Interview with Adm.S. 6th & 21 Divisions to arrange that men transferred to 1st Corps Rest Station (Acc.) should bring all clothing & equipment with them — owing to the difficulty of stock here owing to the necessity for replacing deficient clothing from units today. —	AMcR
LABEUVRIERE	25/7/17		Routine post — without sunshine — nothing unusual to report. — Case of Pte WIEGOLD. 14 Durham Light Infantry — admitted 24th. Dog bite — investigated — found that dog has been killed — owner of dog unknown — Body of dog head been sent to Mons. AVERSNOY. Veterinaire. GONNEHEM. near CHOCQUES for examination. Intense cold still continues.	AMcR
LABEUVRIERE	26/7/17		Intense cold still continues	AMcR
LABEUVRIERE	27/7/17		Pte WIEGOLD. G. 14 DLI. left this morning for treatment at (Pasteur) at Debrulin Hôpital des Cochinidres, PLAINE, ST DENNIS, PARIS. — brilliant sunshine —	AMcR
LABEUVRIERE	28/7/17		First still sunshine — Slight attack of flu in the Brevet 1st Corps Rest Station A.S.C. men g to decline defect in Flue — key lost damage done. —	AMcR
LABEUVRIERE	29/7/17		Severe frost — still continues — brilliant sunshine	AMcR

Army Form C. 2118.

WAR DIARY
or
INTELLIGENCE SUMMARY

(Erase heading not required.)

74 Field Ambulance. 79.

Place	Date	Hour	Summary of Events and Information	Remarks and references to Appendices
LABEUVRIERE	30/1/17	—	Frost still continues. Keen air - sky clear - brilliant sunshine.	AN Roe Major
LABEUVRIERE	31/1/17		Frost still severe - Clear sky - Casco of Pyrexia numerous - Nothing unusual to report.	AN R Major

A.N. Roe
Lt Col.
OC 74 Field Ambulance.

140/199

24th Div.

74th Field Ambulance

COMMITTEE FOR THE
MEDICAL HISTORY OF THE WAR
Date 4.— APR. 1917

Army Form C. 2118.
80

WAR DIARY
or
INTELLIGENCE SUMMARY

(Erase heading not required.)

74 Field Ambulance

Vol 17

Place	Date	Hour	Summary of Events and Information	Remarks and references to Appendices
LABEUVRIERE	1/2/17	-	Frost still continues - nothing unusual to report -	Aurore Star
LABEUVRIERE	2/2/17	-	Principal Catarrh very prevalent amongst other ranks. Great as patients. - Severe frost. -	AMR
LABEUVRIERE	3/2/17	-	Handover Capt A.R. KING-RAINE, on proceeding on leave. Severe frost. Sunshine.	DRK'n
LABEUVRIERE	4/2/17		Presentation by C.O. to Corpl. Commander, of ribbons gained recently. M.M. - A/Sgt. To dd A. R.A.M.C. awarded M.M.	BRK
LABEUVRIERE	5/2/17		Slight fall of snow overnight. Severe frost with bright sunshine. Nothing unusual to report.	DRK.
LABEUVRIERE	6/2/17		Frost continues, much trouble with cars. Slight increase in sickness amongst neighbouring troops.	DPK
LABEUVRIERE	7/2/17		Hard frost, clear bright sunshine. Inspected of field Amb. Station. All Satisfactory.	DRK

Army Form C. 2118.
81.

WAR DIARY
or
INTELLIGENCE SUMMARY

74 Field Ambulance

(Erase heading not required.)

Place	Date	Hour	Summary of Events and Information	Remarks and references to Appendices
LA BEUVRIERE	8/2/17		Severe frost. Roads very hard for horse traffic. Nothing unusual to report.	D.R.V.
LA BEUVRIERE	9/2/17		Frost continues. Chloride of lime carrier invented by D.D.M.S. 1st Corps passed to 74th & 2nd Fd. for inspection report. Capt. G.S. PIRIE. R.A.M.C. proceeded to 73rd F. Amb. for temporary duty. Posted to 18 Ces struck off the strength of Capt. H.J. McCURRICH, R.A.M.C. (T.C.)	D.R.V.
LA BEUVRIERE	10/2/17		The unit from this date authority (D.M.S. P.C. 8/3/15 dated 6-2-17.) Frost still continues. Health troops very good during the day.	D.R.V.
LA BEUVRIERE	11/2/17		Severe frost. Roads had m horses cars nothing to report	D.R.V
LA BEUVRIERE	12/2/17		Frost continues. Shortage of forage movement difficult	D.R.V.
LA BEUVRIERE	13/2/17		Frost continues but temp slightly higher. C.R.S. inspected by D.D.M.S. 1st Corps	D.R.V.
LA BEUVRIERE	14/2/17		Slight thaw today. Concert given in recreation hall 1st Corps Troupe "very light". Attended by Corps General A.D.M.S. & 24th Division	D.R.V.

Army Form C. 2118.

WAR DIARY
or
INTELLIGENCE SUMMARY

(Erase heading not required.)

74 Field Ambulance

82.

Place	Date	Hour	Summary of Events and Information	Remarks and references to Appendices
LABEUVRIERE	15/2/17		Lt. Col. A.M. ROSE. A.D.S.O. R.A.M.C. Returned from leave to duties acting A.D.M.S. while Col. BUSWELL A.M.S. is on leave to ENGLAND.	D.R.16.
LABEUVRIERE	16/2/17		2 officers 1 OR of 74th F.A.M.B. attended inspection by Gen. NIVELLE of the FRENCH ARMY. Weather clear, bright frost.	D.R.16
LABEUVRIERE	17/2/17		Cloudy day. Scabies still continuing. Nothing unusual to report. (One) Scabies amongst Ambulance personnel.	SCM
LABEUVRIERE	18/2/17		Corps Rest Station, inspected by BRIG. GEN. B.R. MITFORD. C.B. D.S.O. temporarily commanding the 24th Div. Infective diseases tending to increase in the area. Cloudy day, damp underfoot.	ARM
LABEUVRIERE	19/2/17		Nothing unusual to report. CAPT. W.M. BIDE M. R.A.M.C.(SR) LT. COOK R.A.M.C. (T.C.) reported for temporary duty.	D.R.16.
LABEUVRIERE	20/2/17		Heavy rain all day. CAPT. W.M. BIDEN R.A.M.C.(SR) proceeded to 73rd F. Amb. for duty.	D.R.16.

2449 Wt. W14957/M90 750,000 1/16 J.B.C. & A. Forms/C.2118/12.

WAR DIARY
INTELLIGENCE SUMMARY

74 Field Ambulance

Army Form C. 2118.
83

Place	Date	Hour	Summary of Events and Information	Remarks and references to Appendices
LA BEUVRIERE	21/2/17		Nothing unusual to report. Infectious diseases especially measles, rather more frequent	DRM
LA BEUVRIERE	22/2/17		Nothing unusual to report. Weather continues	DRM
LA BEUVRIERE	23/2/17		No 76 Rev 375 S.S Major Riley J.P. C. returns to Divisional train. Reorganetic no struck off the strength. Weather raw.	DRM
LA BEUVRIERE	24/2/17		Weather damp raw. Nothing unusual to report. P.S.M. Pearce R.A.C. reports to temporary duty	Still DRM
LA BEUVRIERE	25/2/17		Corps Rest Station inspected by A.D.M.S. 1st Corps. Nothing unusual to report. Weather milder.	DRM
LA BEUVRIERE	26/2/17		Nothing unusual to report. Weather milder.	DRM
LA BEUVRIERE	27/2/17		Nothing unusual to report. Bathing room for patients finished for C.R.S.	DRM

Army Form C. 2118.

WAR DIARY
or
INTELLIGENCE SUMMARY

74 Field Ambulance

84

(Erase heading not required.)

Place	Date	Hour	Summary of Events and Information	Remarks and references to Appendices
LABEUVRIERE	28/2/17		Nothing unusual to report — 1st C.F.S. (A'see) very full — measles rather prevalent.	McRae Lt Col

McRae
Lt Col
O.C. 74 Field Ambulance

74th Field Ambulance

24th Div.

140/20

COMMITTEE FOR THE
MEDICAL HISTORY OF THE WAR

Date 11 MAY 1917

Army Form C. 2118.

WAR DIARY
or
INTELLIGENCE SUMMARY
(Erase heading not required.)

74 Field Ambulance

Vol 18

Place	Date	Hour	Summary of Events and Information	Remarks and references to Appendices
LABEUVRIERE	1/3/17	—	O.C. Corps Reat. Station AIRE handed over to 72 Field Ambulance. Weather mild and sunshine at intervals.	Apx R. Attatchne Apx R.
LABEUVRIERE	2/3/17	—	Measles still occuring in various units in the Division —	
LABEUVRIERE	3/3/17	—	Admis: returns for leave. — Column 2 Officers + 35 O.R. proceeded to-day to take over adv. dressy Station at AIX NOULETTE fm 3 Canadian Field Ambulance. — Adv: party fm 72 Field Ambulance arrived LABEUVRIETE to take over 1st Corps Reat. Station A2ee.	Apx R.
LABEUVRIERE	4/3/17		Main party 74th Field Ambulance left LABEUVRIERE at 8 a.m. route via FOUQUEREUIL, FOUQUIERE, VERQUIN, NOEUX-LES-MINES, PETIT SAINS — to school at CITE 10 — (FOSSE) Map Ref. (36.B) — R.8 central. — an hot meal was fm 3rd Canadian Field Ambulance arriving 12 noon. —	Apx R.
FOSSE 10 PETIT SAINS	5/3/17		Cleaning Station — to visit — visits Advanced Dressing Station was No 4 RAVIC Post on SOUCHEZ Road.	Apx R.

WAR DIARY or INTELLIGENCE SUMMARY

Army Form C. 2118.

74 Field Ambulance

Place	Date	Hour	Summary of Events and Information	Remarks and references to Appendices
Fosse 10.	6/3/17		Weather cold - heavy rain - all work proceeding. - Gas Alert On.	Arthur Lean
Fosse 10.	7/3/17		Inspection of Dressing Station by D.D.M.S. 1st Corps and Inspecting A.D.S. Ramc. proto by A.D.M.S. 1st Division - Measles prevalent among troops	M.R.
Fosse 10.	8/3/17		Weather very cold. - Snow. - All improvements proceeding. - Measles still prevalent.	M.R.
Fosse 10.	9/3/17		Inoculation This Coll. - Snow at intervals -	M.R.
Fosse 10.	10/3/17		Inspection of Dressing Station by A.D.M.S. 1st Division. - Two cases of Measles sent today.	M.R.
Fosse 10.	11/3/17		Weather much milder - both R.A.M.C. bearer units very busy owing to German raid on our lines - necessitating (carrying) wounded over open ground under heavy shell and machine gun fire. Owing to damp German weather trenches rendering this impossible.	M.R.

Army Form C. 2118.

WAR DIARY
or
INTELLIGENCE SUMMARY

(Erase heading not required.)

74 Field Ambulance. 87.

Place	Date	Hour	Summary of Events and Information	Remarks and references to Appendices
Fosse 10.	12/3/17	—	Weekly inspection of men for P.B. duty by O.B. & 24 Divisn at H.Q. Unit. Inspection of Advanced Dressing Station by A.D.M.S. — no fresh cases of weather mild — some rain — Quiet night — no wounded brought in — All improvements to H.Q. Continues.	Lt Col R.A.M.C. Officers
Fosse 10.	13/3/17		Nothing unusual to report. — Weather milder — some rain — Lt. Harris Revd. to lightly duty with 9 R. Sussex Regt.	M.v.R.
Fosse 10.	14/3/17		Inspection by A.D.M.S. 24 Divisn — with men to establish dressing station at "Walking wounded" en route to be followed by Motor Cars Convoy from A.D.S. Aix-Noulette. —	M.v.R.
Fosse 10.	15/3/17		Nothing unusual to report — Visited A.D.S. Aix-Noulette. — no wounded during tonight. — no wounded cases —	M.v.R.
Fosse 10.	16/3/17		Inspection of Dressing Station by D.D.M.S. 1st Corps — weather dry — night quiet — no wounded cases.	M.v.R.
Fosse 10.	17/3/17		Nothing unusual to report. — no cases of wounded —	M.v.R.
Fosse 10.	18/3/17		Conference of A.D.M.S. and Sub. Amb. Commanders — regarding evacuation of walking wounded.	M.v.R.

Army Form C. 2118.

WAR DIARY
or
INTELLIGENCE SUMMARY

(Erase heading not required.)

74 Field Ambulance. 88.

Place	Date	Hour	Summary of Events and Information	Remarks and references to Appendices
JOSSE E.10.	19/3/17		Weather cold and windy - Some rain. - Acc improvements to main Dressing Station and A.D.S. Continued	Am.Rze. St.ese.
JOSSE 10.	20/3/17		Nothing unusual to report. - Wind very high. Coes. road at intervals	AmR
JOSSE 10.	21/3/17		Inspection of transport by O.C. 24 Divisional Train. -	Am R.
JOSSE 10.	22/3/17		Weather Fine. cold. - Nothing unusual to report.	Am R.
JOSSE 10.	23/3/17		Inspection of A.D.S. - Nothing unusual to report. Weather still cold.	Am R
JOSSE 10	24/3/17		Inspection of Dressing Station by A.D.M.S. 24 Division - Weather Clear and cold - brilliant sunshine - Lt. GAY. 16th Squadron R.F.C. brought in wounded. 6 p.m.	Am R
JOSSE 10.	25/3/17		Lt. GAY. died at 6 a.m. - -	Am R.

Army Form C. 2118.

WAR DIARY
or
INTELLIGENCE SUMMARY.   74 Field Ambulance

(Erase heading not required.)

Instructions regarding War Diaries and Intelligence
Summaries are contained in F. S. Regs., Part II.
and the Staff Manual respectively. Title pages
will be prepared in manuscript.

Place	Date	Hour	Summary of Events and Information	Remarks and references to Appendices
Fosse 10.	26/3/17		Weather cold aw bad. - Nothing unusual to report	Hulme Frz Myl
Fosse 10.	27/3/17		All improvements continues. -- Return for admits & in/outs.	Myl
Fosse 10.	28/3/17		21 wounded arrives during the night - two been begins in Division	Myl R
Fosse 10.	29/3/17		Nothing unusual to report - Weather the Coldest. Most. -	Abst
Fosse 10.	30/3/17		Lieut Cochrane leaving on furlough -	Myl
Fosse 10.	31/3/17		Nothing unusual to report - Weather still cold -	Myl

Hulme
Major
OC 74 Field Ambulance

140/2086

24th Div

74 F.A.

April 1917

COMMITTEE FOR THE
MEDICAL HISTORY OF THE WAR
Date −6 JUN. 1917

Army Form C. 2118.

WAR DIARY
or
INTELLIGENCE SUMMARY.
(Erase heading not required.)

74 Fd Ambulance JF/F/19

Place	Date	Hour	Summary of Events and Information	Remarks and references to Appendices
JOSSE 10. PETIT SAINS	1/4/17		Nothing unusual to report. - Trench shelters are hot - several casualties arrived during the night.	Mc Rae Lieut Name
JOSSE 10.	2/4/17		Brewing Station an ADS. at Av. NOULETTE inspected by Lt. Gen. HOLLAND CB, DSO Commanding 1st Corps - Considered enemy artillery activity round ADS. - One HE. shell exploded in courtyard of ADS. - no casualties - Weather cold. Snow at intervals	Lou. R.
JOSSE 10.	3/4/17		Nothing unusual to report. -	ShuL
JOSSE 10.	4/4/17		At 10.7pm the Horse Lines bivouacs were shelled by two enemies - 1 civilian killed and 1 wounded	ShuL
JOSSE 10.	5/4/17		At 3.30 pm German shell burst near hospital. 1 man RFA killed + 5 RFA wounded. - 2 french civilian wounded.	Muy AuR
JOSSE 10.	6/4/17		Nothing unusual to report. Weather still cold. - No 1 Banic Post Evacuates into temporary ADS. hotels. unusual to report -	MR Banic Post Evacuates
JOSSE 10.	7/4/17		Preparation for Meeting of walking wounded S.	ShuL
JOSF 10	8/4/17		Visit by a Bring to ADS. and No. 1 Post -	ShuL

Army Form C. 2118.

WAR DIARY
or
INTELLIGENCE SUMMARY.
(Erase heading not required.)

74 Field Ambulance

Place	Date	Hour	Summary of Events and Information.	Remarks and references to Appendices
JOSSE 10	9/4/17	—	Day relatively quiet — Admitted 50 stretcher bearers sent up to A.D.S. — Being night bearers — Casualties occurred in Gun pit near Dressing Station. 7 men badly hurt — dresses — and evacuated to C.C.S.	A/RO Roz Lieut
JOSSE 10	10/4/17		Another Explosion occurred in Gun pit of Heavy Battery — 3 cases brought in, two of whom were badly burned - face & hands —	A/nR.
JOSSE 10	11/4/17		Day fairly quiet — Preparation continuing for reception of wounded — 110 beans at A.D.S. and Relay Posts — four Medical Officers — 1 M.O. Catching Range with Stretcher parties, 1 M.O. Capt Faulkner with at H.Q. 1 Relay Post (Railway Trench) This Medical Officer's (Capt Davidson & Capt Atkin) at A.D.S. — At Main Dressing Station preparation for receiving wounded Cupboards — Rack bins and Dressing Room — with Have an buffet (Cocoa + sandwiches) - pyjamas - and Dressing Room — with Six Dressers under Capt Wallace Ranie.	A/nR.
JOSSE 10	12/4/17		Attack by portion of Divn. on Enemy at 5.30 am. — Wounded began to come in about 8.30 am. — and Continues all day. — Totals to 6 p.m. — Officers . 8 — O.R. 174 —. — Almost entirely Rifle or M.G. Bullet wounds	A/nR.

2353 Wt. W2514/1454 700,000 5/15 D.D.&L. A.D.S.S./Forms/C. 2118.

Army Form C. 2118.

WAR DIARY
or
INTELLIGENCE SUMMARY.
(Erase heading not required.)

74 Field Ambulance (92)

Instructions regarding War Diaries and Intelligence Summaries are contained in F. S. Regs., Part II and the Staff Manual respectively. Title pages will be prepared in manuscript.

Place	Date	Hour	Summary of Events and Information	Remarks and references to Appendices
JOSSE 10.	13/4/17		Nothing unusual to report – weather still cold.	Mr Rose sick
JOSSE 10.	14/4/17		At 5 p.m. Enemy shells bursting in front of unit heavily – A. Block damaged – No Casualties. Evening patrols at Hennuelle – Shelley Curtius for an hour –	Mr R.
JOSSE 10.	15/4/17		73rd Bde Infantry advancing thro ANGRES – LIEVIN – towards LENS – Some artillery in support, tried with Reg Aid Posts and evacuation of wounded over K. Slate of Ground – Bad for Cars in S. Kits. – Bodies of A.D.S. to Cafe Negrier best route for evacuation of wounded. – Capt King R.A.M.C. with shelter parties laying bugle on Road. –	
JOSSE 10.	16/4/17		Visited A.D.S. – Capt Barclay R.A.M.C. investigating barrier routes for evacuating casualties. – A.D.S. Established by Capt King, at which Chalet LIEVIN.	
JOSSE 10.	17/4/17		Weather bad – Wounded being evacuated from LIEVIN by Wheel Stretchers on tram road from LIEVIN to A.D.S. 73 Field Amb. CALONNE and thence by cars of this unit to JOSSE 10.	
JOSSE 10.	18/4/17		Visited A.D.S. of 73rd Field Amb. and 74 Field Amb. at LIEVIN – Shelled in Chapel of Chalet, together with Reg Aid Post of 13 Middlesex Regt & 12 R. Fusiliers	

Army Form C. 2118.

WAR DIARY
or
INTELLIGENCE SUMMARY.
(Erase heading not required.)

74 Field Ambulance (93)

Instructions regarding War Diaries and Intelligence Summaries are contained in F.S. Regs., Part II. and the Staff Manual respectively. Title pages will be prepared in manuscript.

Place	Date	Hour	Summary of Events and Information	Remarks and references to Appendices
Josse 10	18/4/17	Cultures	Route to LIEVIN by light railway track – running thro' to LIEVIN from BULLY-GRENAY – lines we installed for evacuation of wounded by mule-drawn Trolley. – Entrance (only) for N. Midland Fees Ambulance arrived at Josse 10 – an Advance Pouty for no. 3 N. Midlws Fees Aut arrives Aix-NOULETTE to take over.	An Ros Ster Remi
Josse 10	19/4/17		A.D.S. at LIEVIN taken over by no. 3 N. Mid. Field Ambulance – an A.D.S at Aix-NOULETTE by same unit. – Detachment of to wink at LIEVIN and Aix-NOULETTE return to H.Q at Josse 10.	An R
ECOUEDECOURS	20/4/17		Unit. left Josse 10 at 9 am having handed over to 1st N. Midland Fees Ambulance tracks via HERSIN – BARLIN – MARLES-LES-MINES – AUCHEL – BURBURE – LILLERS – arriving ECOUEDECOURS at 6 pm. – Men marches well – weather fine. Roads good – horses into billets – Our presence in barns – Horses under cover in stables.	An R
ECOUEDECOURS	21/4/17		Weather dull, rather cold. – Capt Cabin raise Allen in which were to Regimental Brewing area. – Scrutein of village billets.	

Army Form C. 2118.

WAR DIARY
or
INTELLIGENCE SUMMARY.

(Erase heading not required.)

74 Field Ambulance

Instructions regarding War Diaries and Intelligence Summaries are contained in F. S. Regs., Part II. and the Staff Manual respectively. Title pages will be prepared in manuscript.

Place	Date	Hour	Summary of Events and Information	Remarks and references to Appendices
ECQUEDECQUES	22/4/17	—	Men resting — Divine Service 11 am — weather still cold, no rain	Thy Roe Lieutenant
ECQUEDECQUES	23/4/17	—	Men resting — Advance party to LISBOURG — for billets —	Thy R
LISBOURG	24/4/17	—	Left ECQUEDECQUES at 9 am. route via AMES, RIMETTES - PALFART - arrived LISBOURG at 3 pm. — weather cool + no rain — men heavily weld — Billets in Schools + barns	Thy R
LISBOURG	25/4/17	—	Men resting — School converted into Dressing Station for 17 Infantry Brigade	Thy R
LISBOURG RCQUEDECQUES	26/4/17	—	weather cool but fine — Left LISBOURG at 2 pm — route via PALFART - WESTREHEM. - ST HILAIRE - LES PESSES - arriving ECQUEDECQUES 7 pm.	Thy R
BETHUNE.	27/4/17	—	Left ECQUEDECQUES at 2 pm route via LILLERS - CHOCQUES - arriving BETHUNE at 6 pm — took over billets of Casle au Military Hospital — men in billets — weather cool - no rain —	Thy R
BETHUNE	28/4/17	—	weather cool — arrangements made by O.C. to establish a Dressing Station for each of 17th Infantry Brigade	Thy R

Army Form C. 2118.

WAR DIARY
or
INTELLIGENCE SUMMARY.
(Erase heading not required.)

74 Field Ambulance

Instructions regarding War Diaries and Intelligence Summaries are contained in F.S. Regs., Part II. and the Staff Manual respectively. Title pages will be prepared in manuscript.

Place	Date	Hour	Summary of Events and Information	Remarks and references to Appendices
BETHUNE	28/4/17	—	Arranging collection of sick for units of 7th Infantry Brigade — Arranging Hospital Accommodation — weather have billeted sunshine —	Mr. Rees Scot. Accee.
BETHUNE	30/4/17	—	Handed over command of 74 Field Ambulance to Capt. F. C. Davidson. N.C. Rouen for midnight 30 April — 1st May —	Mr. Rees
BETHUNE	1/5/17	1pm	Took over command of 74th Field Ambulance vice Lieut Col A. Scott. R.A.M.C. Div. No 107/88 A/30.4.17. [signature] Capt. R.A.M.C. OC 74 Field Ambulance. Took over command of 74th Field Ambulance from Lt Col A. Scott D.S.O. Relief to D.D.M.S. Meerut (Antrobus) R.A.M.C. Divi. No 107/88. Spring's and accounts found correct and in order. 2 Motor Vans to admit 125 wounded. Ambulance wagons and car (loan) wagons furnished. Arrived patients to clear their patients from Regimental aid posts to collect.	[signatures]
BETHUNE	2/5/17	—	Weather rain then warm. Sunshine.	
BETHUNE	3/5/17	—	Weather warm. Arranging Officers lead in hospital. Amb transport wagons and Cars (no heavies) ready for work. Each car an 8 cwt 10cwt car. Patient nursing in hospital.	

COPY.

B.E.F.

SUMMARY OF MEDICAL WAR DIARIES of

74th Field Ambulance,

24th Division,

1st Corps, 1st Army, till 21.4.17.
2nd Corps, 1st Army, from 21.4.17.-10.5.17.
2nd Corps, 2nd Army, from 10.5.17.

WESTERN FRONT, APRIL - MAY, 1917.

O.C. Lt.Colonel A. M. Rose, till 30.4.17.
Capt. F. C. Davidson, from 30.4.17.

SUMMARISED UNDER THE FOLLOWING HEADINGS:-

Phase "B" - Battle of Arras. "April - May, 1917."

1st Period, April 1917. Attack on Vimy Ridge.

2nd Period, May, 1917. Capture of Siegfried Line.

74th F.A., 24th Division B.E.F. Western Front.
O.C. Lt.Col. A. M. Rose. April 1917.
1st Corps, 1st Army. 1.

Phase "B" - Battle of Arras. "April - May, 1917."

1st Period, April 1917. Attack on Vimy Ridge.

April	
	H.Q. at Fosse 10, Petit Sains.
1st	Casualties "Several during night".
2nd	Med. Arr. A.D.S. - Aix Moulette.
	Operations Enemy. Artillery activity round A.D.S.
4th	Operations Enemy & Casualties Fosse and vicinity shelled. 1 killed and 1 wounded, civilians.
5th	Operations Enemy & Casualties Shell burst near Hospital. 0 & 1 killed, 0 & 5 W. R.F.A. 2 French civilians W.
9th	Med. Arr. 0 & 50 Brs. to A.D.S.
	Accident & Casualties Explosion in gun pit of Heavy Artly. 0 & 7 wounded.
10th	Accident & Casualties A second explosion in gun-pit of H.A. 0 & 3.
11th	Med. Arr. 4 & 110 at A.D.S. and R.A.M.C. Posts.
12th	Operations Attack by portion of 24th Divn. at 5.30 a.m.
	Casualties First arrived at 8.30 a.m.
	Total 8 & 174 W.
14th	Operations Enemy. H.Q. of unit heavily shelled 5-6 p.m. "A" block damaged. No casualties.
15th	Operations & Evacuation 73rd Inf. Bde. advanced through Angras - Lievin towards Lens.
	Some difficulty in getting into touch with R.A.P's and in evacuation of W. owing to state of ground.
17th	Evacuation From Lievin by Wheeled Str. on main road from Lievin to A.D.S. 73rd F.A. Calonne.
	Light Railway between Liévin and Bully Grenay.
19th /	

74th F.A., 24th Division, B.E.F.   Western Front.

O.C. Lt.Col. A. M. Rose.   April 1917.

1st Corps, 1st Army, till 21.4.17.   2.
2nd Corps, from 21.4.17.

Phase "B", continued.
1st Period, continued.

April	H.Q. at Fosse 10, Petit Sains.
19th	Med. Arr. A.D.S. Liévin taken over by 3rd N. Mid. F.A. with A.D.S. Aix-Noulette.
20th	Moves To Ecquedecques.
21st	Transfer To 2nd Corps Area.

74th F.A., 24th, Division B.E.F.   Western Front.

O.C. Lt.Col. A. M. Rose, till 30.4.17.   April 1917.
      Capt. F.C.Davidson, from 30.4.17.
      2nd Corps, 1st Army.   3.

Phase "B", continued.
1st Period, continued.

April		
	H.Q. at Equedecques.	
21st	Transfer	To 2nd Corps Area.
24th	Moves	To Lisbourg.
26th		To Ecquedecques.
27th		To Bethune.
30th	Appointment	Capt. F. C. Davidson to O.C. 74th F.A. vice Lt.Col. Rose to Rouen.

74th F.A., 24th Division B.E.F.   Western Front.
O.C. Lt.Col. A. M. Rose.   April 1917.
1st Corps, 1st Army.   1.

Phase "B" - Battle of Arras. "April - May, 1917."
1st Period, April 1917. Attack on Vimy Ridge.

April	
1st	H.Q. at Fosse 10, Petit Sains. Casualties "Several during night"
2nd	Med. Arr. A.D.S. - Aix Moulette. Operations Enemy. Artillery activity round A.D.S.
4th	Operations Enemy & Casualties Fosse and vicinity shelled. 1 killed and 1 wounded, civilians.
5th	Operations Enemy & Casualties Shell burst near Hospital. 0 & 1 killed, 0 & 5 W. R.F.A. 2 French civilians W.
9th	Med. Arr. 0 & 50 Brs. to A.D.S. Accident & Casualties Explosion in gun pit of Heavy Artly. 0 & 7 wounded.
10th	Accident & Casualties A second explosion in gun-pit of H.A. 0 & 3.
11th	Med. Arr. 4 & 110 at A.D.S. and R.A.M.C. Posts.
12th	Operations Attack by portion of 24th Divn. at 5.30 a.m. Casualties First arrived at 8.30 a.m. Total 8 & 174 W.
14th	Operations Enemy. H.Q. of unit heavily shelled 5-6 p.m. "A" block damaged. No casualties.
15th	Operations & Evacuation 73rd Inf. Bde. advanced through Angras - Lievin towards Lens. Some difficulty in getting into touch with R.A.P's and in evacuation of W. owing to state of ground.
17th	Evacuation From Lievin by Wheeled Str. on main road from Lievin to A.D.S. 73rd F.A. Calonne. Light Railway between Lievin and Bully Grenay.
19th	

74th F.A., 24th Division, B.E.F.   Western Front.

O.C. Lt.Col. A. M. Rose.   April 1917.

    1st Corps, 1st Army, till 21.4.17.   2.
    2nd Corps, from 21.4.17.

Phase "E", continued.
1st Period, continued.

April	
19th	H.Q. at Fosse 10, Petit Sains.
	Med. Arr. A.D.S. Liévin taken over by 3rd N. Mid. F.A. with A.D.S. Aix-Noulette.
20th	Moves To Ecquedecques.
21st	Transfer To 2nd Corps Area.

74th F.A., 24th Division B.E.F.   Western Front.

O.C. Lt.Col. A. M. Rose, till 30.4.17.   April 1917.
　　　Capt. F.C. Davidson, from 30.4.17.
2nd Corps, 1st Army.   3.

Phase "B", continued.
1st Period, continued.

April		
	H.Q. at Ecquedecques.	
21st	Transfer	To 2nd Corps Area.
24th	Moves	To Lisbourg.
26th		To Ecquedecques.
27th		To Bethune.
30th	Appointment	Capt. F. C. Davidson to O.C. 74th F.A. vice Lt.Col. Rose to Rouen.

COMMITTEE FOR THE
MEDICAL HISTORY OF THE WAR
Date 10 JUL. 1917

140/2161

No. 74 F.O.

Army Form C. 2118.
96.

WAR DIARY
of
INTELLIGENCE SUMMARY. 76th Field Ambulance.

Vol 20

(Erase heading not required.)

Instructions regarding War Diaries and Intelligence Summaries are contained in F.S. Regs., Part II and the Staff Manual respectively. Title pages will be prepared in manuscript.

Place	Date	Hour	Summary of Events and Information	Remarks and references to Appendices
BÉTHUNE.	1/5/17		Took over Command of 76th Field Ambulance from midnight 30th April – 1st May. Lt. Col. A.M. ROSE. D.S.O. R.A.M.C. Departs to rejoin O.D. No.5. ROUEN. Bombardment of town from 6.30 – 8 – 2 Civil venks wounded. Several civilians wounded. Few killed. Avis de fait automobiles to move their patients from hospitals. Wards to cellars. Weather fine. Warm, bright sunshine.	[signature] Capt.
BÉTHUNE	2/5/17		Weather again fine – very warm. Annoying present stille in hospital – transport wagons and lorries recommended. Again fine weather. Arranged these rand in hospital. Auto mover.	[signature] Capt.
BÉTHUNE	3/5/17		2 Civil patients in hospital 22. LIEUT. BENT. R.A.M.C. reports for duty. Shells fire in town between 9 and 9.30 p.m. – Removed all civilian patients to cellars. Treated few civilian wounded. Fine weather continues. Air hospitals. CAPT R.W. MACPHERSON. R.A.M.C. taken on strength of this unit from 3.5.17. [Auth AR No 268 of/3.5.17.]	[signature] Capt.
BÉTHUNE.	4/5/17		CAPT. M. M'KNIGHT. R.A.M.C. S.R. stuck of strength from 4.5.17. [Auth ARs AD.m.S. 2nd Div. LIEUT. T.F. WINDSOR. R.A.M.C. T.C. AND CAPT. A.C. FERR. R.A.M.C. (R.) reports for duty. 10 6m 8/5/17.] Some bombs dropped on town 9.30 pm. Civil patients in hospital 25.	[signature]

WAR DIARY
INTELLIGENCE SUMMARY. 74th Field Ambulance

Army Form C. 2118.

Place	Date	Hour	Summary of Events and Information	Remarks and references to Appendices
BETHUNE	5/5/17		Fine weather continues – LIEUT. J.F. MORGAR. R.A.M.C. (T.C.) departs for U.K. via 73rd F.A.	J.C. Marshm
BETHUNE	6/5/17		Continuation of fine weather. CAPT. MORTIMER. R.A.M.C. reports on return to CAPT. R.E. BROWN. M.O. i/c 1st ROYAL FUSILIERS, on leave. Ambulance cars - 9am - arrived at 0.31. G.S.S. (Point 36A. 1/20.000) 2.15 pm and took our MALANOY FARM from filled parties to 73rd F.A. 75 skin patients - units sections taken over. (Operation order No 106. R.O.M.S. 24th Div.)	J.C. Marshm
MALANOY FARM	7/5/17		Continuation of fine weather. Arranging hospital – general fatigues. Battalion parade. Established canteen for men who have no facilities for purchasing goods in town. Visit of R.O.M.S. 24th Div. and D.D.M.S. II Corps.	ggs
MALANOY FARM	8/5/17		Rain this forenoon. Fine afternoon. Arranging instruments re disinfectors. Arranging Recplan Divide Disinfector to scabies Market. Clubs. balls. etc. CAPT. FAULKNER. L.D. R.A.M.C. taken on strength of this unit from 6.5.17.	ggs
MALANOY FARM	9/5/17		Ambulance moved at 2pm to ROBECQ. (1/J.T.R. O.O. No 153. and R.A.M.C. O.O. 107. 23 Patients accompanied unit. accompanied in R.A.M.C. 2a Div.) Battalion of Royal ambulance cars. In khaki. Fine weather.	ggs
ROBECQ	10/5/17		Continuation of fine weather. Cleaning of kit. Arranging Medical Inspection Room. Camp ? Bd. W.O. admitted. Parties Continuent no? leaves necessary. Reports to R.O.M.S. to reassemble ? Div. and D.D.M.S. 2n Div.	ggs

WAR DIARY

INTELLIGENCE SUMMARY

Army Form C. 2118.

7th FIELD AMBULANCE

Place	Date	Hour	Summary of Events and Information	Remarks and references to Appendices
HAZEBROUCK	11/5/17		Unit departs for POPERINGHE at 9 am. - morning to HAZEBROUCK. Arrangements made for ambulances to accompany battalions of Brigade on march. Capt J. Butler returns to 10/5/17 - R.A.M.C. personnel on ambulances by the first trains. Ambulances billeted in two farms. Officers bivouac'd. Beautiful weather.	
STEENVOORDE	12/5/17		Unit departs from HAZEBROUCK 7am. - arrived STEENVOORDE 10.50 am. Very warm - and fine. Ambulance wagons accompanied battalion on march. Billets in town - good accommodation. Officers billeted in town.	
STEENVOORDE	13/5/17		Fine weather. Foot washing parade. Arranging hospital. Advance Party & "C" Section and 2 officers went forward to take over Camp at POPERINGHE - from No 133 Field Ambce. (under instruction from A.D.M.S. 2a Div.)	
STEENVOORDE	14/5/17		Fine weather continues. Men's foot parade enforced now by next and 2nd bathing. Nothing unusual to report.	
POPERINGHE	15/5/17		Left STEENVOORDE 5.30 am. marched via ABEELE to POPERINGHE - arriving 8.30 am. at ST. STANISLAS COLLEGE. RUE DE BOESCHEPE. (sheet 28. G.7.b.8.8.) Afternoon spent in general fatigue - cleaning up wards, quarters - relieving found etc. Difficult in finding beds. Standings - burial of Clinical CAPT C NAPIER RAMC TO struck off strength of unit - SKT to 96 Field Ambce Corpl H.----- no further.	
POPERINGHE	16/5/17		Arranging hospital and reception room.	

WAR DIARY or INTELLIGENCE SUMMARY.

Army Form C. 2118.

74th FIELD AMBULANCE. Sheet 99

Place	Date	Hour	Summary of Events and Information	Remarks and references to Appendices
POPERINGHE	17-5-17	—	Raining heavily. Costs. In hospital officer 1, other ranks 20. A.D.M.S. visited hospital. 3 R.A.M.C. orderlies and 6 T.V. men deleted fr Wake Point G.	Appendix Cap
POPERINGHE	18-5-17	—	Under A.A.M.S. instructions this hospital is considered with Divisional Rest Station from today's date. R.C. Rel. Capts. visited. Indispute internits fr h.C. — JOSEPH SMETS — 1st SERGEANT — Belgian. Inspector of water carts – R.E. wagons, ambulance wagons + limbers.	App
POPERINGHE	19-5-17	—	Fine weather. Ample hospital accommodation for hospital. Enable 2 men attended hospital – R. 20 O.R. Evacuated for A/C rule 72nd F.A.	App
POPERINGHE	20-5-17	—	Fine weather. Interpreter train/send to 73rd F.A. Nothing to report.	App
POPERINGHE	21-5-17	—	Costs. rain in evening and overnight. Continued work of nursing attention breaker – and SGT. ADIES. R.A.M.C. relieved by A/S.S.M. MCRAMS. R.S.E. from Cape.	App
POPERINGHE	22-5-17	—	Rain in morning – fine afternoon. Critical medal – officer + men. Total patients in hospital 87. Payment of rents – and attached of "Snipers" Divisional Gas School.	App
POPERINGHE	23-5-17	—	Fine weather. Brakast evacuation of patient members 6 t. "p" in 3-n days to C.C.S. Enemy shelled town between 6h - 6.45p. – no casualties. CAPT. MORTIMER. b. forwarded to 166 R.E. R.E.M. for temporary duty.	App
POPERINGHE	24-5-17	—	Continuation of fine weather. Total patients in hospital 79. Evacs. have fm 7h-6.17, 6h-6.17, 6h-6.17 – no casualties. Handed over temporary charge of Unit to CAPT. J.R.KING. R.A.M.C of this ambulance.	App Cap

Army Form C. 2118.

WAR DIARY
or
INTELLIGENCE SUMMARY

(Erase heading not required.)

No 6 Field Ambulance

Sheet 100

Place	Date	Hour	Summary of Events and Information	Remarks and references to Appendices
POPERINGHE	25/5/17		Capt. F.C. Davidson RAMC proceeded on leave to England. The Field in which the Fr Amb is bivouacking shelled last night & this morning	DAL6
		1.T + Q.M.	LT. + Q.M. W.S.C. MERRYMAN, R.A.M.C. att. 74th F. Amb. was severely injured, his left leg being blown off just above the ankle. He might he received injured two stretcher	
			2 [And] was carried today because the convent was shelled again at	
		6. A.M.		
			No 14512 PTE SORBY, J.C. R.A.M.C. att. 74th F. Amb. was slightly wounded but remained at duty. The casualties in the Fr Amb units around us were few in number but serious in nature.	
IN THE FIELD	26/5/17		Lt. G.C. HARTLEY R.A.M.C. proceeded on temporary duty to 68th BUFFS	DAL6
P.O.C.S.6. WARLIS.			Nothing of interest to report — weather improving.	
	27/5/17		Weather hot & strong sunshine. Inspection front 9.30 nothing of interest to report.	DAL6
	28/5/17		Strong sunshine again. Nothing of interest to report.	

WAR DIARY
or
INTELLIGENCE SUMMARY.

2nd "A" Field Ambulance. Page 101

Army Form C. 2118.

(Erase heading not required.)

Place	Date	Hour	Summary of Events and Information	Remarks and references to Appendices
G.20.C.6.4. SHEET 28	29.5. 17		Inspected some R.A.P.s in 41st Divisional area today, not enough protection against shell fire & still higher than the parapet of trench. Accommodation poor.	D.D.M.S.
G.20.C.5.6. SHEET 5.46	30.5. 17		Weather good; health of men excellent. CAPT A.C.JEBB R.A.M.C. with 6.S.T. proceed by post to H.Q. 138th F. Amb for instructions. Made a reconnaissance of the forward area	D.D.M.S.
G.20.C.S.Q. SHEET 28	31.5. 17		F. Amb moved today to X Corps training area at K.15.c.2.1 SHEET 27. for the reception F.Amb from 17th Inf Brigade.	D.D.M.S.

Carbons

B.E.F.

SUMMARY OF MEDICAL WAR DIARIES of

74th Field Ambulance,

24th Division,

1st Corps, 1st Army, till 21.4.17.
2nd Corps, 1st Army, from 21.4.17.-10.5.17.
2nd Corps, 2nd Army, from 10.5.17.

WESTERN FRONT, APRIL - MAY, 1917.

O.C. Lt.Colonel A. M. Rose, till 30.4.17.
      Capt. F. C. Davidson, from 30.4.17.

SUMMARISED UNDER THE FOLLOWING HEADINGS:-

Phase "B" - Battle of Arras. "April - May, 1917."

1st Period, April 1917. Attack on Vimy Ridge.
2nd Period, May, 1917. Capture of Siegfried Line.

74th F.A., 24th Division B.E.F.   Western Front.

O.C. Capt. F. C. Davidson.   May 1917.

2nd Corps, 1st Army, till 10.5.17.
2nd Corps, 2nd Army, from 10.5.17.

Phase "B" - Battle of Arras. "April - May, 1917."

2nd Period, May 1917. Capture of Siegfried Line.

May		
1st	H.Q. at Bethune.	
	Operations Enemy & Casualties	Bethune bombarded 6.30 - 8.
	0 & 2 W. Several civilans killed or wounded.	
3rd		Bethune bombarded.
4th		"Some bombs" on town.
5th	Moves	To Malanoy Farm.
10th	Moves & Transfer	To Robecq, en route for 2nd Army.

74th F.A., 24th Division B.E.F.　　　　　　Western Front.

O.C. Capt. F. C. Davidson.　　　　　　　　May 1917.

    2nd Corps, 1st Army, till 10.5.17.　　　1.
    2nd Corps, 2nd Army, from 10.5.17.

Phase "B" - Battle of Arras. "April - May, 1917."

2nd Period, May 1917. Capture of Siegfried Line.

May		
	H.Q. at Bethune.	
1st	Operations Enemy & Casualties	Bethune bombarded 6.30 - 8.
	O & 2 W. Several civilans killed or wounded.	
3rd		Bethune bombarded.
4th		"Some bombs" on town.
5th	Moves	To Malanoy Farm.
10th	Moves & Transfer	To Robecq, en route for 2nd Army.

140/2230

No. 74. 7.a.

COMMITTEE FOR THE
MEDICAL HISTORY OF THE WAR
Date - 7 AUG. 1917

19 D.A. & Q.M.S

24th Division

Attached please find original
War Diaries for month of
June 1917, of 74th Field Ambulance

[signature]
Lieut. Col. R.A.M.C
Officer Commdg. 74th Field Ambulance

Army Form C. 2118.

WAR DIARY
of
INTELLIGENCE SUMMARY.
(Erase heading not required.)

74th F.A. Field Ambulance.

Place	Date	Hour	Summary of Events and Information	Remarks and references to Appendices
K15.C.3.1. SHEET 27	1/6/17		Weather fine, health of troops good. Nothing of interest to report. Made a reconnaissance of the forward area to-day.	DRM
K15.C.3.1. SHEET 27	2/6/17		Weather continues fine. Nothing of interest to report.	DRM
K15.C.3.1. SHEET 27	3/6/17		Weather still fine. Wind turned today from K15.C.3.1 to G.20.C.5.6 in the cool of the evening. Made a reconnaissance of the forward area today.	DRM
G.20.C.5.6 SHEET 28	4/6/17		Weather still fine. Nothing of interest to report.	DRM
G.20.C.5.6 SHEET 28	5/6/17		Relieved from line. — Lewis' noted at 12 midnight to M.S.O. until. Phew 28. Arranged for ambulances per lorry to wait in rear of this area. Made a reconnaissance of forward area and saw A.D.S. to be at Brae. Unit was carrying wars. Eight numbers VI(light) and 2(sit) lorries for the bearers flooded up — his bearers below orders stopped about mid-way between 12 bearer men (11 Otr. 15 Pt) Sam Bairensen. Bearer captain left to carrying point at 12 pm. 5 Car Ambulance corps sent to report to O.C. 73rd F.A. Bearer sub-division left to carrying point at 5 pm. Runners & Bear Brewer. CAPT. P.L. PELLY. R.A.M.C. reported for duty. Orders Ang. 75. 13th F.A. and arranged rate O.C. bearers until ordered their to carry engage — from 1.15.113 to thin M.D.S.	
M.S.O. Curb	6/6/17		3 Motor Ambulances sent to D.S.C. & A.D.S. 138 F.A. Weather fine.	

Army Form C. 2118.

Sheet 103

WAR DIARY
INTELLIGENCE SUMMARY
(Erase heading not required.)

No. 3 3rd Aus. Amb. MCE

Place	Date	Hour	Summary of Events and Information	Remarks and references to Appendices
3rd Canadian Sheet 28	8/6/17		CAPT. D.B. KING. R.A.M.C. of this unit killed in action 7/6/17. PTE. HEWITT. A.E. R.A.M.C. — do — do — 7/6/17. PTE. HARGREAVES. F. B.A.M.C. wounded. Fine weather. Debit area has continued. Stretcher wounded being collected and D of E. [illegible] slight in comparison with relief to [illegible]. Went over the heavy section this morning and saw [illegible] [illegible] reg.[?]	JHM / Capt
3rd Canadian Sheet 28	9/6/17		LT. BELLAMY. A.F. R.A.M.C. reports for duty. Visits advanced post, light railways being restored — and [illegible].	Jas
3rd Canadian Sheet 28	9/6/17 morning No. 619		Advanced Dressing Station mated — also Capt. Fitzes and Capt. Faulkner. B.C. relief known also in the line. CAPT. WHITTINGHAM. No. 3/1 C.A.M.C. reports for duty 9/6/17 — on return of this unit hospitals — taken on medical charge of C.A.M.C. — Casu.[?] assn of this unit.	Jas
3rd Canadian Sheet 28	10/6/17		LT. BELLAMY detailed to take charge of No. 3 Post from this date.	
3rd Canadian Sheet 28			PTE. MILNE. G. R.A.M.C. A [illegible] reports wounded — 7/6/17. CAPT. SKENE. L.H. R.A.M.C. T.O. attached to this unit for d.d. Visits No. 3 Pot and Central Post[?] in at 6 p.m. Bryant (17th) relieved in evening.	Jas
3rd Canadian Sheet 28	10/6/17		Dull day, light snow. Arranged relief of men the battalions in rests. A.E. [illegible] (Brew) relieved — No. 3 Post vacated. CAPT. SKENE. L.H. detailed for duty at hq. C.[?] — vice CAPT. F.E. PELLY — returned to this unit.	Jeff
3rd Canadian Sheet 28	10/6/17		2 officers — 200 O.R. detailed to proceed to T.M.O. E.R.A. as working party for R.O.E. and C.R.A.E. hq. in front. Visits R.A.P. cele[?] half in conn'n[?] with evil road — light railway of line & road to C.E.S.[?]. Fair morning — Thunder and heavy rain in evening.	Jas
			LT. KELWOOD. W.A. & LT. T.E. WALKER. U.S. Medical Service reports for duty.	Jas

Army Form C. 2118.

WAR DIARY
of
INTELLIGENCE SUMMARY.
(Erase heading not required.) 74th FIELD AMBULANCE.

Sheet No 66

Place	Date	Hour	Summary of Events and Information	Remarks and references to Appendices
M.S.D. Coulté Sheet 28	13/6/17		Meet Authorities (Consular - 2 (British) Division) involved & I.W.C. 57 & related A.D.S. This have subdivision detailed under Capt. Peters and Capt. Fawsitt to take over as A.D.M.S. bearer posts - and to reinforce R.A.P.s. Divisional Board (2 Lt. M. V. O.R.) out to act as telegraph men on light railways. Fine weather. Very warm.	J.R. Macneile Capt.
-do-	14/6/17		Visits A.D.S. & P.A.s. All equipment completed. Relief Field Ambs. & Field Co. Divers. Drew horse at 7.30 this night.	Jeff
-do-	15/6/17		Another parade twice today. 2 sect 9 NCOs & 2 NCOs & 5 Cav. (A.D.M.S., No. 15/3 - A/3.6.17) Report received from A.D.S. LHS Canadian Infy - as usual arrangement - all ranks satisfactory.	Jeff
-do-	16/6/17		Visits A.D.S. - and arranged for all emergency personnel etc. will own from A.D.S. C Relief P.H.B. Fine warm weather. Difficulty is being experienced in finding a new site for M.D.S. and is also divisional area.	Jeff
-do-	17/6/17		Withdrawal of emergency personnel - 41 O.R. return to M.O. Continuation of fine weather. 1st Lt. Kellogg - U.S.R. detailed to Infirmary M.D.S. Mos. 7 W.F.B.	Jeff
-do-	18/6/17		Reid selected of site for M.D.S. in M.T. camps - tent cars sent to divisional Rest Station - New leaving A.D.S. at I.25 C.2 Sheet 26 and name gmf at Bluff I. 33.d.8. 1st Lt. Warner U.S.R. detailed to A.D.S. to W. Lister. General Stoner (Firm) R.A.M.C. released U.S.R. 1st North Staffs Regt. Vice R. Rent Regt. while wounded.	Jeff

Army Form C. 2118.

Sheet 105

WAR DIARY
of
INTELLIGENCE SUMMARY.
(Erase heading not required.) 2/1st FIELD AMBULANCE

Instructions regarding War Diaries and Intelligence Summaries are contained in F. S. Regs., Part II. and the Staff Manual respectively. Title pages will be prepared in manuscript.

Place	Date	Hour	Summary of Events and Information	Remarks and references to Appendices
Wn.S.D Castle Sheet 28.	19-6-17		Heavy rain during night – and morning. Arranged relief of Officers, N.C.O's men in trenches, posts and dugouts. Unhealthy part of line because of continual heavy rain.	Appendices etc
— do —	20-6-17		Rain, rain, rain, this interval. An order for Bearers unit to 70th F.A. – also sent home 36 bearers of this unit attached to him for duty.	do
— do —	21-6-17		Heavy rain. Visited M.D.S. Two casualties occurring – Personnel being relieved every four days. Total casualties of this unit since 7th inst – are 2 killed (1 officer 1 O.R.) 7 wounded (2 O.R.) of which 3 remained on duty, 1 sick referred to duty, 3 evacuated etc.	do
— do —	22-6-17		Nothing to report. Weather still better. Some rain.	do
— do —	23-6-17		Evacuated reliefs of personnel in trenches. Posts – fine – no rain.	do
— do —	24-6-17		More settled weather. Nothing to report – Hun aeroplane activity very marked.	do
— do —	25-6-17		Improved weather.	do
— do —	26-6-17		Fine weather. O.C. 2/1st Field Amb. called – and arranged reliefs & taking over of M.D.S. and posts.	do
— do —	27-6-17		Fine weather. Advanced parties 2/1st F.A. arrived at M.D. Transport marched 4.15 p.m. 3 days trek to Rest area. Capt. Tebbs and 70 R.A allotted transport to 2/3/1.F.A. who entrained for Rest area Advance Billets party (1 Sgt. 1 Cpl) sent by ambulance car to be billets for Squadron Area of 2/3/2.1.F.A. Handed our M.D.S. Worthoul down to 96th Field Ambulance.	do
— do —	28-6-17		Fine weather. Handed over all M.D.S. posts to 2/1st Field Ambr. 23rd Division – and also M.S.D. centres. Also O.R. – all personnel of this unit returned to M.D.S. and roads to our Bivouacs to Rest area with 2/1st F.A. by train.	do

Army Form C. 2118.

WAR DIARY
of
INTELLIGENCE SUMMARY. 7th Field Ambulance.
Sheet No. 1

(Erase heading not required.)

Instructions regarding War Diaries and Intelligence Summaries are contained in F. S. Regs., Part II. and the Staff Manual respectively. Title pages will be prepared in manuscript.

Place	Date	Hour	Summary of Events and Information	Remarks and references to Appendices
M.O. Outing	29.6.17		Handed over M.O. duties to 21 Fd. Ambulance. 23 Division. Unit entrained 3 fr. with half of 175 F.B. for LUMBRES 8.15 pm. Halted for night — good accomodation —	
LUMBRES Hut 53.Rendezvous				
ALINCTHUN Hut C.5.M.C.	30.6.17		Unit marched 8 am. on way to ALINCTHUN — to RUMETCRUN — Detains 17 miles. rain and fog — arrived 4.15 pm. billeted in Ch[au] FRESNOY — very comfortable. Not Cine — Durring the last months the General has had a great deal of hard work to perform — as Medical head in the gross. Casualties have fortunately been slight — but his new regime & good work health of personnel has remained (excellent).	

[signatures]
O.C. 7 Fd. Amb.

COMMITTEE FOR THE
MEDICAL HISTORY OF THE WAR
Date   10 SEP. 1917

Army Form C. 2118.

WAR DIARY
of
INTELLIGENCE SUMMARY. 74th Field Ambulance
(Erase heading not required.)

Instructions regarding War Diaries and Intelligence Summaries are contained in F. S. Regs., Part II. and the Staff Manual respectively. Title pages will be prepared in manuscript.

Place	Date	Hour	Summary of Events and Information	Remarks and references to Appendices
WIMEREUX Nr. CALAIS	1-7-17		Arranged hospital accommodation in new area. Can accommodate 50 patients. Have billeted in Upr. Wimereux in civilian "Patras" in tents. Beach for swimming. Weather dull and cool. Personnel resting.	
do	2-7-17		Arranged bus routes to points of furthest interest: Nesles, Ferring Pass, Wissaut & A.D.M.S. weather improved. 4/LT REEVES Co. U.S.A. temp. attached 12th Sherwood.	
do	3-7-17		Fine weather. R.M.S. special inspect. adding routine.	
do	4-7-17		Training continued.	
do	5-7-17		4/LT WALKER V.T.R. proceeds to 8th N'PERS for Lewis gun inst. LT. V.M BROWN R.M. & R.M.C. reported for duty.	
do	6-7-17		Fine weather. Bathing at night. CAPT. C.D. FOULKNER transferred to 64th Average to Lightly inf. LT. CRAWFORD R.M. proceed to Britisk RC for permanent Staff via CAPT G.E FARR R.M. reported here for duty. Taken on strength 5-7-17. Fine weather.	
do	7-7-17		Continuation of training. Unit meets being arranged for friendly. 9th inst. Fine warm day. Visit of the Baron also same civilian and pleased with improvements made.	
do	8-7-17		Much rain during night - Running patrol - 25.	
do	9-7-17		Mild weather. Church parade.	
do			Sports Day. Dull weather. Arrangements made. Except: CPL. LEE - winner of gymnast. Factories. Visit Mr. Inspector Seaside.	
do	10-7-17		Fine weather. Routine of duties permits, continued. Limited number of passes to Boulogne Grands rock & for churches & cafes. LT. BELLAMY R.P. of this unit (presented in 3rd R.Mil.) now Capt. Permanent now opp - Taken on by 3rd R.M.S. and is struck off strength accordingly.	
do	11-7-17		Fine weather. Sea bathing.	
do	12-7-17		Circus afternoon. Continuation of fine weather. Nets kept.	
do	13-7-17		Brigade Sports. This unit compete several events - no prize.	

Army Form C. 2118.

WAR DIARY
of
INTELLIGENCE SUMMARY.
(Erase heading not required.) 7th to Field Ambulance —

Sheet 108

Place	Date	Hour	Summary of Events and Information	Remarks and references to Appendices
Alincthun Pas de Calais	14-7-17		Fine weather. Nothing unusual to report.	J. Moseley
— do —	15-7-17		Church service. Divisional cadre B.G.C. 7/13 at night.	Major RAMC
— do —	16-7-17		Arrangements being made for move to new areas. Several of patients to C.C.S. in Cars.	do
— do —	17-7-17		Unit moved to Lumbres. Han. Brigade (17/1/13) moving to Lumbres area. Billets poor.	do
Lumbres Point 50 Hazebrouck	18-7-17		Remaining in Lumbres. Accompanied 73/1/13 search to Renescure area. Large number of sick (suspected diarrhoea) from battalion. Diarrhoea in troops is epidemic not infectious.	do
Renescure	19-7-17		Unit moved to Renescure area. Accompanied 73/1/13. to Caestre area. Ambulance moved with men bygad - 17/E/13. Billets poor.	do
Caestre	20-7-17		Moved to Caestre with 17/E/13. Accompanied 73/1/13 - to Eecke area. Good billets in Fields and Farms.	do
Eecke	21-7-17.		Moved to Eecke with 17/E/13. Billets good. Advanced party - 1 officer - 5 O.R. Lieut Cornell left from 71st Field Ambulance at Reninghelst.	do
Steenvoorde	22-7-17		Moved to Steenvoorde with 17/E/13. B. Trains in fields - enl Farmers.	do
Reninghelst	23-7-17		Moved to Reninghelst - heavy Column over from 71st Field Ambulance.	do
— do —	24-7-17		Fine weather. Advanced bearer posts (10 pm, 20 OR) proceeded to support C.C.S.	do
			7th Field Ambulance Collecting posts from 73rd + 17th Inf. Bns. and Corps Imp —	
— do —	25-7-17		Have many sick inspected. Brig.-Genl. William Division Surgeon inspected N.P.s at zone 8. Sheet 2.8.	do
			Fine weather. Brig.-Genl. William Division Surgeon inspected H.Q. 7th F.A.	

Army Form C. 2118.

WAR DIARY
of
INTELLIGENCE SUMMARY.
(Erase heading not required.) 7th (Field) Ambulance. Sheet 1. 128.

Instructions regarding War Diaries and Intelligence Summaries are contained in F.S. Regs., Part II. and the Staff Manual respectively. Title pages will be prepared in manuscript.

Place	Date	Hour	Summary of Events and Information	Remarks and references to Appendices
ENINGHELST	26/7/17		Tent Sub Division - "B" & "C" Sections to Inf. & Corps Main Dressing Station at M.C.A.S.T. (Sheet 28).	J. Mould.
-do-	27-7-17		47. ANDREW known to refunds to Infantry D.S. Fine weather. Enemy aircraft dropped bombs at 11 pm - no damage to hospital. few casualties.	JMcK
-do-	28-7-17		Fine warm weather. Area Commanders visits hospital and advised further "screening" of all tents. Patients unusual to infantry.	JM
-do-	29-7-17		Rain & thunder. Nothing to report.	JM
-do-	30-7-17		Rain - dull.	JM
-do-	31-7-17		Rain day. Rain stopped in late afternoon. "Zero hour" 3.45 am this morning - beginning of march - Reg. 107. The health of hosp. has been exceptionally good. On the first half of month the hosp (adv) was in rest - and during this we served into camp a breakdown occurred, portable hospital, very largely to change of surroundings, food etc.	JM, JMcK, home O.C. 7th C. Field Ambulance

31/7/17.

JMould
O.C. 7th C. Field Ambulance.

140/364

No. 74. 7 a.

Aug. 1917

COMMITTEE FOR THE
MEDICAL HISTORY OF THE WAR
Date −1 OCT. 1917

WAR DIARY
of
INTELLIGENCE SUMMARY

(Erase heading not required.)

Vol 23

74th Field Ambulance. (Sheet 109)

Place	Date	Hour	Summary of Events and Information	Remarks and references to Appendices
EWING HUTS.	1/8/17		Very wet – and dull. Nothing unusual to report.	Appendix
Sheet 28. 36.C.20J	2/8/17		Noon mean: Lt. D.W.L. ANDREW proceeded to take over of Bearer Division of this unit. Noon max. Large number of Private details. M.I.R. but not many admissions.	App. j
Do	3/8/17		Noon max. – Noon min 2. 7.V.D. and repeated benches sent from Ets. Drugs: "C top" visits in French post – "nips in huts"	App. j
Do	4/8/17		Fair. Pris internal.	App. j
Do	5/8/17		Lowest case of 7.107 fever but no as lowest fever – paterive and trials at altitude absent in order of trial. Nothing to report. Reserve in account of "pickness" nil.	App. j
Do	6/8/17		Nil to report. Dull showery weather.	App. j
Do	7/8/17		Nothing to report. Fair weather except for thunder shower in evening. Lt. ANDREW this unit returned to us. Commenced to build grass huts for stretcher cases.	App. j
Do	8/8/17		1st Lt. HAMMEL H. MORE, U.S.A. reported for temporary duty. Fair weather.	App. j
Do	9/8/17		Heavier R.E. materials for such I. Dry afternoon.	App. j
Do	10/8/17		Birds Outfits during night – casualties line ?. Wind S.E. Did grounds Li. wounded S.	App. j
Do	11/8/17		Morn rain – midafter – mid Midday. Drainage of camp well for hrs. line Nothing unusual. After G 13 hrs Gabeless shells went – returning to trenches because rest after.	App. j
Do	12/8/17		Fine morning – rain in afternoon. On ambulance found to be suffering from disabilities	App. j
Do	13/8/17		Nolling to report. Warm Clear.	App. j
Do	14/8/17		Nole to report – warm & mid. Lt. STEVENS proceeded on 14 days Combat leave to England.	App. j
Do	15/8/17		Fine indicate – warm rain. Capt. JEBB – M.O.V.C. this unit returned to this unit relieved by Lt. ANDREW.	App. j
Do	16/8/17		Nothing to report.	App. j

Army Form C. 2118.

WAR DIARY
INTELLIGENCE SUMMARY. 74th. FIELD AMBULANCE. Sheet 51D.

(Erase heading not required.)

Place	Date	Hour	Summary of Events and Information	Remarks and references to Appendices
EINNEKERKE	17/8/17		Capt. McTIGGS returned & takes up duty as D.D.M.S. 2 Corps	
Do	18/8/17		Weather & reports fairly much the same. Wind allowing M.I.R. duty - chiefly rest for Coys and army fr. Tps. Dumbarton to forwards driver not impossible in light. Due to firemen's fatigue.	
Do	19/8/17		Bomb dropped at 9.30 pm - No Casualties - Fine weather - and benefit change of tp. 3 to 6 tom wounded night - (1 ND, 1 LD, 1 2 DIV). 6 Ambulance trips sent to workshop for repair.	
Do	20/8/17		Bomb dropped in neighbouring camp - few casualties - 2 funerals afternoon and 2 confirmed Corps wounded to Spot Cpl. Sick morning in IP 203 -	
Do	21/8/17		Fine weather. Sick & dying norm nearly completed. LT. VERLOGA Start on "Special" leave fr. 21 - 26 - to England.	
Do	22/8/17			
Do	23/8/17		Fine weather. Gas alarm from the evening - calm - nothing occurred - nothing to report. Fine day -	
Do	24/8/17		Rev. FOSTER R.C of M.C. S/Scts etchs. and M.C. R.C. Mines. 6.75 Dio. Wind - and showers.	
Do	25/8/17		Fair weather. Nothing to report.	
Do	26/8/17		Dull weather - not rain -	
Do	27/8/17		Rainy during night. Notes on M.I. Rawlings 6 men fr. O.S. at 8.20 a.m. Nothing to report.	
Do	28/8/17		LT. MOREN started for Company Infr on hrs 8th BUFFS - vice LT. WINDOW. R.M.C. V. Strong wind - hurt but from Every night - Rain. LT. VERLOGA USA returned fr.	
Do	29/8/17		Variable weather continues - leave. On care of officers, enlistment and nr. can of children for admin. This and Sacraments	
Do	30/8/17		LT. ILOTT. R.M.C. vis. refused for D.C.	
Do	31/8/17		nothing to report.	

COMMITTEE FOR THE
MEDICAL HISTORY OF THE WAR
Date —5 NOV. 1917

Army Form C. 2118.

WAR DIARY
or
INTELLIGENCE SUMMARY
(Erase heading not required.)

FB/16

Vol 24

14th F.A.
R.A.M.C.

WAR DIARY / INTELLIGENCE SUMMARY

Army Form C. 2118.

Sheet. III.

74th FIELD AMBULANCE.

Place	Date	Hour	Summary of Events and Information	Remarks and references to Appendices
C34.6.6'0. Sheet 28.	1/9/17		USA. Lt. Kerwood visits as usual. RE, RE2'(?) Div. into 27 WARWICKS Ramps to 72nd F.A.	Appendix 12 [?] Files
— do —	2/9/17		Lt. Cosens. RAMC T.C. attached for duty may help. Capt. Beaumont RAMC this unit returns from leave.	Jeff
— do —	3/9/17		Lt. Kerwood USA. man cancelled. Bomb dropped [?] during night. returned wounded total 31. Sent to [?] (medical officer's [?]). From time to time [?] enemy aeroplanes in front of line [?]. Reporting visits of A.P. Dumps last night - calico substituting glass.	Jeff
— do —	4/9/17.		Fine weather. Officers visits keep [?] - against bomb attacks.	Jeff
— do —	5/9/17.		Fine weather. Nothing to report.	Jeff
— do —	6/9/17.		Capt. C.J. FAULKNER R.A.M.C. this O.C. - a repair [?] [?] - of England.	Jeff
— do —	7/9/17.		Nothing to report.	Jeff
— do —	8/9/17.		Fine weather. Nothing to report. Making so [?] (medical wounds) J.	Jeff
— do —	9/9/17.		Returned 1 Sgt. and 10 men to 72nd F.A. Attached 1 Sgt. 29 O.R. [?] for same purpose.	Jeff
— do —	10/9/17.		Fine weather. Continuation of [?] [?] matter.	Jeff
— do —	11/9/17.		Lt. Col. Bunch RAMC has [?] [?] in 10 days leave to England. Continuation of fine weather.	Jeff

WAR DIARY / INTELLIGENCE SUMMARY

Army Form C. 2118.

No. to Field Amb. C.E.   Sheet No. 112

Place	Date	Hour	Summary of Events and Information	Remarks and references to Appendices
A.24.b.2.d. Sheet 28.	11/9/17		Nothing to report. Arrangements being made for his suspending train to Morris area. Strength return asked for by "authority".	Appendix
—Do.—	12/9/17		S.O. Wrellis handed Gros Knords — on to Br. 3rd F.A. Rain during night — Cool.	Yes.
—Do.—	14/10/17		Packing up — preparing to transfer to new area.	Yes.
—Do.—	15/9/17		Advance party of 1 Offr. & O.R. from 3rd Australian Div. take over preview of this unit.	Yes.
—Do.—	16/10/17		Unit departs 6:30 a.m. — embussed in lorries & arrives at 7:30 a.m. and proceeded to Morris area (Mazchael Str.) transport proceeding by road under charge of Lt. Hammell U.S.A. Unit allotted in form — 2 barns — Tents for hospital — Offices and Surgeries. Accommodation (?)	Yes.
F.2.a.c.8. Red 36A	—Do.—		Resting — No work kept arterin' and succession of Brigade Side'. Weather this and warm.	Yes.
—Do.—	17/9/17		Nothing to report. Weather favorable — Critical failure — rain.	Yes.
—Do.—	18/9/17		Nothing to report. Some showers — later rain.	Yes.
—Do.—	19/9/17		Dull morning. Turning to Australian at noon. Packing up.	Yes.
—Do.—	20/9/17		Entrained 20/9/17 midnight — pretends 5 hours (1 team + luth'—7 9/1 Major) to ISAMBOMÉ. arrived 2:30 p.m. headed to LECHELLE (P.25. Sheet 57 c.)	Yes.
P.25. Sheet 57 c.	21/9/17		In camp. Weather to report.	Yes.
—Do.—	22/9/17		In camp. Weather to report.	Yes.
—Do.—	24/9/17		Advanced Party under Capt. Bellamy (ma r.) proceeds to Pozières to take over M.D. 104 F.A. Went. A lino to telling on.	Yes.
—Do.—	25/9/17		7 Pts. & escort to infirm Strincles travels Catigny "D" M.S.C. 7 Pts. went. Fine weather.	Yes.

2449 1044 J.B.C. & A. Forms/C.2118/12

Army Form C. 2118.

WAR DIARY
or
INTELLIGENCE SUMMARY
(Erase heading not required.)

7th Br Field Ambulance. Sheet 1/3

Instructions regarding War Diaries and Intelligence Summaries are contained in F. S. Regs., Part II. and the Staff Manual respectively. Title Pages will be prepared in manuscript.

Place	Date	Hour	Summary of Events and Information	Remarks and references to Appendices
Pos. Nov 57c C.23.6. Sheet 62 -do- -do- Sheet 62. Q.28.6.1.5.	26/9/17. 27/9/17. 28/9/17. 29/9/17.		H.Q. F.A. POELCAPPELLE (100 F.A.) and A.D.S. VAPENCOURT, R.16.a,7.5. Sheet 62. Extension of advanced parties on 25/9/17. Remained in present in camp until 27/13. Moved to camp near 17/13. (Sheet 62c C.23.d.) — Advanced parties sent to H.Q. F.A. at POPERINGHE — Q.28.6.1.5. Sheet 62. Whole unit moved to H.Q. POELLY — except 1 officer, 30°2 nursing Co. General site of post. Walk. party injured. A.D.S. ZEANCOURT - advanced party under CAPT. 12677 Rush with a view to taking our these A.D.S. from 73rd F.A. CAPT. PARSONS. W.H. M.C. RAMC. placed permanent in charge to 107 Fd. R.F.A. Continuation of this matter.	[signature] [signature] [signature] [signature] [signature] [signature]
-do-	30/9/17.		Took over A.D.S. ZEANCOURT and R.A.P.s in connection therewith from 73rd F.A. and took over all adjuncts.	[signature]

[signature]
Lieut.
R.A.M.C.
O.C. 7th Field Ambulance.

30/9/17.

"Confidential"
adrian 1/6

40/2499

War Diary
of
14th Field Ambulance
for
October 1917.

Sept 25

COMMITTEE FOR THE
MEDICAL HISTORY OF THE WAR
Date -8 DEC. 1917

Army Form C. 2118.

WAR DIARY
of
INTELLIGENCE SUMMARY

(Erase heading not required.) 76th FIELD AMBULANCE

Page 114

Instructions regarding War Diaries and Intelligence Summaries are contained in F. S. Regs., Part II. and the Staff Manual respectively. Title Pages will be prepared in manuscript.

Place	Date	Hour	Summary of Events and Information	Remarks and references to Appendices
Q.28.d.18.9.				
Shelf C.6.	1/10/17		Continuation of fine weather.	
	2/10/17		Relieved 71st Field Amb. as telling station 200 yards from R.A.S. at Vandencroft Chateau. R.16.6.1.7. Showery. R.E. making to building purposes - also 3 wooden huts in course of erection. Many improvements to the grounds.	J. Kenneth
Do.	3/10/17		Visited all RAPs. ADS in tents. Work progressing satisfactorily. V. few casualties recovery. Fine weather.	Yes
Do.	4/10/17		Weather broke - wind and rain - cases applied for 2000 plank (ceiling, roof and ruin?) for garden.	Yes
Do.	5/10/17		Cases. Some rain - work continues.	Yes
Do.	6/10/17		Resided a day. R.A.M.C. Cafe rides - all work suspended owing to wet. "Concert" at night.	Yes
Do.	7/10/17		Rain - cases. Building operations delayed by inclemency of weather.	Yes
Do.	8/10/17		Rain - V. cold. wind.	Yes
Do.	9/10/17		Some rain. Work continues in their intervals.	S.M.
Do.	10/10/17		Case fair - Building continuing. Progress slow owing to wet.	Yes
Do.	11/10/17		Rain. Sab to NW. Air works suspended. Except digging in preparation for planking.	Yes
Do.	12/10/17		Rain. Sab to NW. Do. Do. work & report.	Yes
Do.	13/10/17		Improvement in weather conditions. V. windy. NW. wind - visited A.D.S. Seaforth. and purposes road leading to RAPs with a view to establishing relay posts to facilitate evacuation of "dying" cases in wet weather.	Yes
			First performance of Yellow 73rd - "Concert party" v. successful. Witnessed by A.D.M.S.	Yes
Do.	14/10/17		Weather improved. Work continued.	Yes
Do.	15/10/17		Fine weather continues. Divisional GOC visits Camp and inspects - continuation of fine weather. Work progressing satisfactorily.	Yes
Do.	16/10/17		Yellow 73rd Concert Party Perform at 73 F.A. 6pm.	Yes

Army Form C. 2118.

WAR DIARY
of
INTELLIGENCE SUMMARY

(Erase heading not required.) 7th. FIELD AMBULANCE. 7

Instructions regarding War Diaries and Intelligence Summaries are contained in F. S. Regs., Part II. and the Staff Manual respectively. Title Pages will be prepared in manuscript.

Place	Date	Hour	Summary of Events and Information	Remarks and references to Appendices
O.C. 7.F.A.	Sept 1917			Page 118
do	17/10/17		Condition of men in malaria unit proves satisfactory.	J.P.Cahir
do	18/10/17		Fine. Nothing to report.	
do	19/10/17		Lt. Col. Dawson O.C. 7th Field Amb. proceeded on ten days leave to Eng. Today. Capt. J. P. Cahir took over Temporary Command.	
do	20/10/17		Nothing to report.	
do	21/10/17		Visited A.D.S at VADENCOURT & JEANCOURT.	
do	22/10/17		Nothing to report.	
do	23/10/17		Very wet day. D.D.M.S 7th Corps inspected A.D.S at JEANCOURT and expressed great satisfaction at its condition owing to the exceedingly bad weather conditions. Field Amb H.Q & A.D.S at Vaden Court were not inspected.	
do	24/10/17		Capt Bellamy relieved Capt Sloan at A.D.S. JEANCOURT.	
do	25/10/17		Very stormy day - Nothing to report.	
do	26/10/17		Nothing to report - had a very good concert this evening - fair progress has been made with training etc during the week.	

WAR DIARY
of
INTELLIGENCE SUMMARY

(Erase heading not required.)

Army Form C. 2118.

74th Field Ambulance Page 116

Place	Date	Hour	Summary of Events and Information	Remarks and references to Appendices
Ourdon Sheet 62.C				
-do-	28/10/17		Visited A.D.S. of JEANCOURT and VADENCOURT - very fine weather nothing to report	J.G.
-do-	29/10/17		Fine weather. Good progress in programme of work	J.G.
-do-	30/10/17		Visited JEANCOURT & VADENCOURT - nothing to report	J.G.
-do-	31/10/17		Returned from leave 30/10/17. Work of construction of huts, hutting &c. has proceeded satisfactorily. A site for new ? has been 3 feet clearly in "buildings" — Camal Park: "Yellow Birds" has performed each first entertainment on fine reception.	Jemmett dim Gen

Jemmett
Lieut.
R.A.M.C.
O.C. 7th Field Ambulance.

31/10/17.

SECRET.

War Diary.
74th Field Ambulance.
Nov 1st To Nov 30th
1917

COMMITTEE FOR THE
MEDICAL HISTORY OF THE WAR
Date   17 JAN. 1918

WAR DIARY or INTELLIGENCE SUMMARY

Army Form C. 2118.

(Erase heading not required.) 7th (i.e. F.S.B.) Yorkshire. Sheet 117.

Place	Date	Hour	Summary of Events and Information	Remarks and references to Appendices
Q.28.d.8.9. Sheet 62.D	1/11/17		Fine weather. Work continuing. Two officers joined the Bn: "Lt. Davis and Lt. Greenway. 6.c. Q.S. more - visited HQrs. Fienvillers - and was shown round at 2.6 Tirencourt.	J Ellemith Lt Col
Do -	2/11/17		Dull foggy weather. Capt. Bellamy of this unit admitted "sick" to Depot. Boones for temporary reliance	J Ett
Do -	3/11/17		Capt. Carrie relieves Capt. Bellamy at HQrs Fienvourt. Visit HQrs Vadencourt. "Yellow Br 7. B 5." B.C. informance in prospect. Continuation of this dear foggy weather.	J Ett
Do -	4/11/17		(Informer) weather. Pontoon made v. 73rd F.A. 72nd D.R.C. - Lost 2-0.	J Ett
Do -	5/11/17		Dull. Some rain.	J Ett
Do -	6/11/17		Work continuing - Nothing further news needs. Capt Bellamy much improved. Capt Williams nominated to perform on 8/11/17 at H.Q. 73rd Div.	J Ett
Do -	7/11/17		Rain all day. Nothing to report. Football match v. 165 Coy RE's and 73rd S.O. afternoon.	J Ett
Do -	8/11/17		Football match v. 166 Bde. R.F.A. Lost 5-2. Nothing to report.	J Ett
Do -	9/11/17		Dull weather. Work continuing. Interupted by rain.	J Ett
Do -	10/11/17		Nothing to report. Concert 6-8 - local attended.	J Ett
Do -	11/11/17		Fine weather. Football v. Sherwood Foresters - Lost 4-0.	J Ett
Do -	12/11/17		Frost - morning - Fine morning - Practise Constructing new - bn competition	J Ett

Army Form C. 2118.

WAR DIARY
of
INTELLIGENCE SUMMARY

(Erase heading not required.) 74th FIELD AMB. C.F. Sheet 118.

Place	Date	Hour	Summary of Events and Information	Remarks and references to Appendices
O.28.11.S.9. Sheet 67.	13/11/19		Men front during night - Cold & windy.	J.L. Manu.
do.	14/11/19		Yellow Book lectures at O.R.C - Cold weather.	" "
do.	15/11/19		Dull tasks day. Nothing to report.	" "
do.	16/11/19		Played hockey v Canadian & Buffs. Fine weather. Yellow Book lectures at Y.M.C.A.	" "
do.	17/11/19		Capt Bellamy of this unit sent to rest for 0.M.O.S. - Dangerous N.Y.D.	" "
do.	18/11/19		Nothing to report.	" "
do.	19/11/19		Visited 12th M.A.C.'s M.I.R. and new R.P. at 25 VERVIERS now complete.	" "
do.	20/11/19		Sick CMS. blister hand N.C.Os and moved to Bonn.	" "
do.	21/11/19		Dull day. Many lectures 6.pm (three hour) - no casualties amg A.T.S's.	" "
do.	22/11/19		Beautiful no other business - hut buildings.	" "
do.	23/11/19		Wet - windy. Nothing to report.	" "
do.	24/11/19		Contracted flu from wet weather. Private Williams T.C. v. Wolf applic (73/76) - drew 0.0.	" "
do.	25/11/19		Hyp.Em. did 6 wounds received this morning. 2 O.Rs also wounded.	" "
do.			Pade Pitethps, Smiths Boud. reports for duty this Unit. Lt. GREENWAY. VSN returned to duty from	
do.			O.R. Sussex.	
do.	26/11/19		Nothing to report.	
do.	27/11/19		Snowfall - sunset hours - colder weather.	
do.	28/11/19		Nothing to report. Improved weather.	
do.	29/11/19		Nothing to report.	
do.	30/11/19		Nothing to report.	

Army Form C. 2118.

WAR DIARY
INTELLIGENCE SUMMARY

(Erase heading not required.) *of* **FIELD AMBULANCE.** Sheet 114.

Place	Date	Hour	Summary of Events and Information	Remarks and references to Appendices
O.B.I.B.Y.	29-11-17		Morning used to prepare to move on 2nd unit.	Jemmaph Kilez
"	30-11-17		Advanced parties (without RAV. F.D. Amb. arrived. Forwards moved by Yellow Bridge. All cars arrived. One cable (with steam indication & equipment) standing by.	Jemmaph Kilez nosmat
			Summary for month - Nothing to report. Except work at F.D. Complete and also at two RDS. Vadrecourt Semicourt.	O.C. 74 F.W. Amba.

No 74. T. A.

COMMITTEE FOR THE
MEDICAL HISTORY OF THE WAR
Date —4 MAR. 1918

WAR DIARY / INTELLIGENCE SUMMARY

Army Form C. 2118.

74 Field Ambulance. Page 120.

Place	Date	Hour	Summary of Events and Information	Remarks and references to Appendices
Q.28.J.8.9.	1/10/17		Old menu cancelled. Own sick in standing to. Pte BLAND H. Rank of this unit awarded M.M. for bravery when carrying in wounded at A.D.S. TERMCOURT.	Appendix
Do.	2/10/17		Fine cold weather. "Stand to".	App
Do.	3/10/17		Forty matches. Nothing to report. Pte "Class L". Pte 23 A.D.S. personnel.	App
Do.	4/10/17		Hard frost one night. Fine day. Pte 103 A.D.S. TERMCOURT.	App
Do.	5/10/17		Outbreak of bad feet.	App
Do.	6/10/17		Continuation of hard frost. Nothing to report.	App
Do.	7/10/17		Birch laying work at Triford and by fire.	App
Do.	8/10/17		Packing up. Preparing to leaving here.	App
BERNES	9/10/17		Handed over H.Q. Personnel & 3rd Cav. F.A. Ambn. A.D.S. TERMCOURT & VADENCOURT to 7th Can. Fld. Ambn. Unit assumed D.E.O. at Dumps BERNES by 73rd F.A. Transport at HAVRECOURT. Took over A.D.S. ROISEL from 2nd F.A. Nothing to report.	App
Do.	10/10/17		Much rain. Lt DAVIS, U.S.A. Detailed as M.O. i/c M.L. SHERWOODS.	App
Do.	11/10/17		V. cold - frost. Nothing to report.	App
Do.	12/10/17		Damp - windy weather.	App
Do.	13/10/17		Nothing to report. Same convoy to 12 R.F.A. at 8.30 pm.	App
Do.	14/10/17		Lt GREENAWAY, U.S.A. detailed to entrain D.S. as M.O. i/c 12 Royal Fus. Everything quiet. With 75 & 23 F.A., we "carry" as this unit is at present occupying accessible forward billets to the centre.	App

Army Form C. 2118.

WAR DIARY
of
INTELLIGENCE SUMMARY

(Erase heading not required.) 74 FIELD AMBULANCE.

Page 124

Place	Date	Hour	Summary of Events and Information	Remarks and references to Appendices
BERNES	15/10/17		Lt. ALDER v.SA. joined as reinforcement. Fine weather.	
do	16/10/17		Hard frost. Nothing to report.	
do	17/10/17		Snow and hard frost - both of clearing work commenced - many snow drifts on roads.	
do	18/10/17		Continuation of frost and snow -	
do	19/10/17		Same weather conditions -	
do	20/12/17		Slight weather conditions. Works MDS ROISEL - much work in progress - repairing billets. Damaged by weather.	
do	21/12/17		Continuation of hard frost. Went to division to arrange for leave.	
do	22/12/17		Lt. BLACK E. v.SA. posted to Company this staff.	
do	23/12/17		Hard frost - snow - nothing to report.	
do	24/12/17		Slight thaw.	
do	25/12/17		Slight thaw - thaw slowly spread & is now pretty general.	
do	26/12/17		Frost again - some rain.	
do	27/12/17		Hard hard hilly thaw. Close 600 horses evacuated of this unit.	
do	28/12/17		Continuation of heavy thaw.	
do	29/12/17		Nothing to report.	
do	30/12/17		Got new car Ford. R.E. material drawn for men's rooms to improve same.	
do	31/12/17		Frost again - nothing to report.	

O.C. 74th Field Ambulance

COMMITTEE FOR THE
MEDICAL HISTORY OF THE WAR

Date -8 APR. 1918

Army Form C.2118.

WAR DIARY
or
INTELLIGENCE SUMMARY 74th FIELD AMBULANCE

(Erase heading not required.)

Sheet No 2.

Place	Date	Hour	Summary of Events and Information	Remarks and references to Appendices
BERNES	1/1/18		Frost - very cold. Men their huts.	J.P. Donaldson
do.	2/1/18		Capt. Carter. RAMC. proceeded on 14 days leave to England. Continued to find accommodation & furnishings to infant.	do.
do.	3/1/18		Nothing to report.	do.
do.	4/1/18		Lt. Duthie R.S. reports to unit - Working party of 30 (military nerv.) sent to A.D.S. Roisel to assist with work in hand.	do.
do.	5/1/18		Lt. Azmer. U.S.A. returned from S.S. C.C.S. - Officers of Brigade on duty have been to struck off strength. Lt. Greenway U.S.A. detailed for temp. any duty with 107th Bde. R.F.A. vice Capt. Parsons. Rome on leave.	do.
do.	6/1/18		Very cold. Had first snowfall. Continuation of snow fall - very cold.	do.
do.	7/1/18			do.
do.	8/1/18		Nothing to report - Three fires and frost.	do.
do.	9/1/18		Visited A.D.S. Roisel - work progressing satisfactorily. Rain all night.	do.
do.	10/1/18		Thaw commencing. Thaw prevention refused. Able to report to Capt. Parsons (Cantor's) Lt. Hammer H.H. USA M.O.R.C. from 15	do.
do.	11/1/18		Thaw continues - nothing to report.	do.
do.	12/1/18		Nothing to report. Snow and slight frost overnight.	do.
do.	13/1/18		Progress of work at A.D.S. Roisel satisfactory. New A.R. machine drawn.	do.

Army Form C.2118.

WAR DIARY
or
INTELLIGENCE SUMMARY

(Erase heading not required.) 74 FIELD AMBULANCE.   Sheet 122

Instructions regarding War Diaries and Intelligence Summaries are contained in F. S. Regs., Part II and the Staff Manual respectively. Title Pages will be prepared in manuscript.

Place	Date	Hour	Summary of Events and Information	Remarks and references to Appendices
BERNES.	14/1/18.		Meeting held by Consult. Surgn V Army – 2.30 p.m. – Subjects :– Shock – fracture included – Demonstration of Thomas' Splints – very instructive.	
Do.	15/1/18.		Rain. Nothing to report. Sent men to reinforcements.	
Do.	16/1/18.		Nothing to report. Gas preventive continues.	
Do.	17/1/18.		"Yellow Birds" performance at 6 p.m. Visits A.D.S. ROISEL – wire fencing ordered. Bullet-riddles for wood submitted.	
Do.	18/1/18.		Nothing to report. Rain – another. "Yellow Birds" again perform to 72nd Inf. Bde.	
Do.	19/1/18.		Capt. J.P. CONVIN attached for Temp. Capt. FAULKNER duties to bell. change. A.D.S. ROISEL. "Yellow Birds" perform –	
Do.	20/1/18.		Very quiet – Some rain.	
Do.	21/1/18.		Rain – nothing to report.	
Do.	22/1/18.		CAPT. C.O. FAULKNER R.A.M.C. proceeded on 14 days A.L. as M.O. i/c 2nd R.B. Regd. held – fine day.	
Do.	23/1/18.		Nothing to report.	
Do.	24/1/18.		Spent morning in "reinforcements" & "catgris" – visits A.D.S. ROISEL – wire fencing satisfactory.	

Army Form C. 2118.

WAR DIARY
INTELLIGENCE SUMMARY

(Erase heading not required.) 7th FIELD AMBCE.

Place	Date	Hour	Summary of Events and Information	Remarks and references to Appendices
BERNES.	25-1-18.		Uneventful this never day.	
Do.	26-1-18.		Quiet day. Work of sandbagging huts on patients & hostile huts and hired the BERNES to BUIRE RD and to Collection headquarters.	
Do.	27-1-18.			
BOISEL.	28-1-18.		Qui matin. Visits by Revd re Div. & DDMS. Can Cope who are selected with progress of work.	
R.16.A.8.1. Sh.62.C.NE.	29-1-18		Cementers found on hand & much 9th & 6th Divs. Commenced herealts. Enjoys them. Also entrance to further tunnel.	
Do.	30-1-18.		Visits by Liem Stroy ADMS who has gone ahead re Lunwad.	
Do.	31-1-18.		Nothing to report. Needs has been spent in building H.O. at ROISIL – weather has improved progress service a.s.	

31/1/18.

O.C. 7th Fd Amb

No. 74. T. A.

COMMITTEE FOR THE
MEDICAL HISTORY OF THE WAR
Date 12 MAY 1918

Army Form C. 2118

WAR DIARY
or
INTELLIGENCE SUMMARY

(Erase heading not required.)

74 FIELD AMBULANCE. Sheet No.

Place	Date	Hour	Summary of Events and Information	Remarks and references to Appendices
Beaulieu K.16.d.R.1.	1-2-18		Capt. H. H. Warner (S.O. proceeds to England) on leave. Weather improving - roads frozen - gun fire by weather.	
do	2-2-18		Reinforcements entrained — 36 men (from 16/1/6 gmen for 6 hours) commence work at back Filienne Tunghaw and Rosses.	
-do-	3-2-18		Visit by 20 O.W. General Commanding who inspected whole place and expressed his approval. Gun weather continues. Lt. Duthie joined this unit from 26[?] [Company?] Dec'd into 73rd Fd. Ambe.	
do-	4-2-18			
do-	5-2-18		Much amusement by plunging fire adjacent to this MO (within 2 secs) Two batteries (mediums & heavies) proceeded to steady Tincourt (or company etc.)	
do-	6-2-18		Nothing to report.	
do-	7-2-18		Some rain. cooler. All firms to Amiens shipped in mud. became to	
-do-	8-2-18		Course of instruction run. Nothing to report. Section of Mess cookhouse.	
do-	9-2-18		Cartmakers to unit on hand — making of baths, refilling attrition rooms, erection of finish shop, etc. Gun weather favors proper fund. Ploughing of ground continued.	
do-	10-2-18		Visit of A.D.C. (Br. Div. G.O.C.) to inspect on holdings. Work continuing — nothing to report.	
do-	11-2-18		Nothing to report.	
do-	12-2-18		Nothing to report — weather remains fine and warm.	

Army Form C. 2118

WAR DIARY
of
INTELLIGENCE SUMMARY.
(Erase heading not required.) 7th FIELD AMBULANCE. Sheet 126.

Instructions regarding War Diaries and Intelligence Summaries are contained in F. S. Regs., Part II and the Staff Manual respectively. Title pages will be prepared in manuscript.

Place	Date	Hour	Summary of Events and Information	Remarks and references to Appendices
K.16.d.8.1. Roisel	13-2-18		Anti-aircraft. Plumbing dismantled may be faster if plugs - knives almost 2 years completed	
do	14-2-18		Anti-aircraft. Rain during night - Butler Report. Portable walk v. 1st Pheasants (2-2).	
do	15-2-18		Cold frosty weather. Work continuing.	
do	16-2-18		Approved visits - and inspects new athletic room. Ord. Orly matter.	
do	17-2-18		Capt N.R. Hammett, Major KCP refuses post W.Ham - declines to proceed. 19/1/18 as no % of Ish Royal Positive. Dent 3rd: troop visits - and inspects HQ. - apparently satisfied.	
do	18-2-18		"Capt. N.R. Hammett (wounded) to 137Bn. R.F. as M.O. Hounds in command (temporary permit) to Capt. J.P. ABNOR - prior to leaving for 1 month leave to England 20/2/18.	
do	19-2-18		Lt. Col. F C Paul returns from leave to England on leave to-day.	
do	20-2-18		Nothing to report.	
do	21-2-18		Cold frosty weather.	
do	22-2-18		Weather very bad - much rain - a re-improvement of six inmates arrived to-day.	

WAR DIARY
or
INTELLIGENCE SUMMARY.

(Erase heading not required.)

Army Form C. 2118.

Place	Date	Hour	Summary of Events and Information	Remarks and references to Appendices
Sheet 62 C K 16 d 8.1	23-2-18		Fine weather. Lieut Greenway H.M. O. U.S.R.C. was posted to Chipilly camp for duty to-day	
"	24-2-18		Medal ribbons were presented to 5 O.R's to-day by the Cav. Corps Commander. Capt Kennedy D.A.D was attached to this Unit, Ambulance to-day for temporary duty within ambulance to report	
"	25-2-16		Fine weather.	
"	26-2-16		Capt Sweeny H.W. M.O U.S.R.C. was attached to this unit to-day	
"	27-2-16		Capt Kennedy was posted to-day for temporary duty until 10th Bde R.F.A. Capt Sweeny H.W. was permanently attached this day to 2nd Cav. Div.	
"	28-2-16		Advance parties were sent to-day to Villers Bretonneux and Chateau Manor in view of the impending move of the Unit. An advance party of 1 Officer + M.O O'Rourke from 2/2 E Lancashire Field Ambulance arrived	

M. Colm W. Feill
Capt RAMC
ag OC 74 Ambulance

140/2902

9th Field Ambulance

COMMITTEE FOR THE
MEDICAL HISTORY
Date -6 JUN 1918

Army Form C. 2118.

WAR DIARY
or
INTELLIGENCE SUMMARY.
(Erase heading not required.)

7th FIELD AMBULANCE   Sheet 17B

Place	Date	Hour	Summary of Events and Information	Remarks and references to Appendices
Sheet 62.C V.5.a.3.7	1/3/18		Orders were received during the night that this unit march to Huvincourt area with 17 I.B. A.D.S. at Ruriel was handed over to 2/2 E. Lancs Field Ambulance. Arrived in new area about 12.30 p.m. Majority of unit accommodated in tents — weather very cold.	J. Baker Capt R.A.M.C.
"	2/3/18		Accommodation improved — advance parties at Villers Bretonneux and Chateau manor were recalled and rejoined on this day. Weather intensely cold.	J.B.
"	3/3/18		Weather still very cold — nothing unusual to report.	J.B.
"	4/3/18		Weather very wet — nothing unusual to report.	J.B.
"	5/3/18		Nothing unusual to report.	J.B.
"	6/3/18		Weather fine and conditions in camp much improved. Lieut Duthie returned to-day from a course of Instruction at the Fifth Army (R.A.M.C.) School. Capt Rev. H. Pickford proceeds to England to-day to report for duty at War Office. Capt Rev. J. H. Eaton Wareham was attached to this Unit to-day.	J.B.
"	7/3/18			J.B.

Army Form C. 2118.

WAR DIARY
INTELLIGENCE SUMMARY.

(Erase heading not required.) 26th FIELD AMBULANCE

Sheet 1/26

Place	Date	Hour	Summary of Events and Information	Remarks and references to Appendices
Sheet 62.C. V5d37	8-3-18		Nothing to report. Weather very fine	JP Leonard Capt
"	9-3-18		An advance party - 2 officers - 5/8 others moved forward to day to Sheet 62.E - STCREPY - for the purpose of preparing a D.R.S.	JMC
"	10-3-18		Capt D A D Kennedy returned from temporary duty with 106 Bde R.F.A and was posted to 3rd Rifle Brigade for duty. 17 Brigade Sports were held to-day and a very enjoyable day spent. Very fine weather.	JMC
"	11-3-18		Nothing unusual to report. Lt Grunsberg was this day attached to No 5 Cas for temporary duty	JMC
"	12-3-18		Capt Andrews P.W.E of this unit was this day attached to 1st Royal Fusiliers vice Capt Hammel H.H. sick. Party proxing St Crew returned to unit to-day	JP
W20 31 Sheet 62.C	13-3-18		This unit moved from Montecourt to Terting to-day and relieved 6th Cavalry Field Ambulance. Accommodation very cramped	JP

Army Form C. 2118.

Sheet 137

WAR DIARY
of
INTELLIGENCE SUMMARY.
7th FIELD AMBULANCE

(Erase heading not required.)

Instructions regarding War Diaries and Intelligence Summaries are contained in F.S. Regs., Part II. and the Staff Manual respectively. Title pages will be prepared in manuscript.

Place	Date	Hour	Summary of Events and Information	Remarks and references to Appendices
Sheet 62.C. W2a31	14-3-18		Time principally occupied in extending Hospital accommodation. Weather very fine	J.H.Baber Capt RAMC
	15-3-18		A bearer Division was formed to-day - ready to move off at a moment's notice - Troops Continued to Camp. D.D.M.S 19 Corps inspected the Camp and suggested some improvements.	JHB
	16-3-18		Nothing unusual to report. A working party of 1 NCO & 9 O.R's was sent to 72nd Field Amb to help in making an A.D.S at Vermand	JHB
	17-3-18		Very fine weather - 1 NCO & 3 nursing orderlies were sent to-day to Fifth Army School (RAMC) of instruction.	JHB
	18-3-18		Capt Hammell H.H. M.O.R.C (U.S.A) was this day evacuated to W 3 4 C.C.S.	JHB
	19-3-18		Nothing unusual to report. Pte Hodgson T. (241993) K O Y.L.I an A.S.C died at 5 C.C.S - result of a kick by one of our mules.	JHB
	20-3-18		Heard unofficially to-day that Pte Hodgson T. (241993) K O Y.L.I an A.S.C died at 5 C.C.S - result of a kick by one of our mules. Weather very wet	JHB

Army Form C. 2118.

Sheet 131

WAR DIARY
INTELLIGENCE SUMMARY
(Erase heading not required.)

Jul 4 Field Ambulance

Place	Date	Hour	Summary of Events and Information	Remarks and references to Appendices
W 2 a 3 1 2/3/18 Stafford	2/3/18		1 Officer & 84 O.Rs were sent to reinforce 72nd Field Ambulance during active operations were in progress.	Kaun
	2/3/18		Early this H.Q. of this unit were relieved by 1/3 Northumbrian Field Ambulance and this unit proceeded to O. 30 C.5.5 (approx) Sheet 62 (C)	fro
O.30.c.5.5.	2/3/18		At 3 a.m. this morning this unit moved from O.30.C.5.5 to T.2.8.t.8.8. (Sheet 62 C).	fro
			At 2-30 p.m. this unit moved from T.2.8.t.8.8. to a Camp about 4,000 yards S.W. of Chauene on the Road to Hallu.	fro
			Early this morning the great majority of our transport/animal from 72nd Field Ambulance	
Chauene			Lieut Col F.C. Davidson arrived from leave of absence & took Command of unit. Ptes Hannan & Seely were to-day officially notified as missing. Ptes Readman & Walker were reported as wounded in action	fro

Army Form C. 2118.

Instructions regarding War Diaries and Intelligence Summaries are contained in F.S. Regs., Part II. and the Staff Manual respectively. Title pages will be prepared in manuscript.

Sheet 122

WAR DIARY
of
INTELLIGENCE SUMMARY.
(Erase heading not required.)

76th FIELD AMBULANCE

Place	Date	Hour	Summary of Events and Information	Remarks and references to Appendices
HALLU. Sheet 62D	26-3-18		Moved from HALLU to LIHONS. Transport to ROSIÈRES Sheet 66E F.9. Established ADS at LIHONS – cars & walking from CHAULNES STA.	J Allmark R H/Lds RAMC
LIHONS. Sheet 62D	25-3-18		Few sick and light wounded evacuated. Walked this morning up to RÓSIERES (Sheet 66E) → CAIX → CAYEUX below and joined transport line. Bearer division arrived tripod 17/18. – Ambulance cars evacuating road. Few walking. Cars fairly right.	Jett
CAYEUX. Sheet 66E D.6.	26-3-18		Established car-post (2 ambulances) on CAIX-VRÉLY road.	Jett
Do	27-3-18		Reason conditions. Had to withdraw car-post in CAIX-VRÉLY road. Supply now & walking (St Casualties)	Jett
ROUVREL Sheet 66E A.3.	28-3-18		Moved to DEMUIN – transport to THEZARD. Fed walking men of which until to ROUVREL	Jett
ST SAULFLIEU Sheet Amiens 7.	29-3-18		Moved from ROUVREL to ST SAULFLIEU – were 1st rest and fed.	Jett
SAINS-EN AMIENOIS Sheet 66E A.2.A.	30-3-18		Moved own to SAINS. Self & adv. party. Rest of Bars DE GENTELLES but walked to SAINS. Cars in task between BOVES and COTTENCHY Road. Established helpless in school at SAINS. Took over ADS at COTTENCHY from 7FA – and which evacuate for divisional (21st) (6LE A.M.B.) 7 mb	Jett
Do	31-3-18		got into Load of 17.72.73 BDes and emerged destitution of casualties – keen to 6-L42. Capt CAHIR detailed as Liason office for Brigade. Capt DUTHIE in charge ADS. Capt TEEN in forward details as M.O. for Infantry Bn. Missing 2 Wounded 7. (Ozt. 2 Smart's). Total casualties reported to date.	J Allmark R Lds Ras RAMC

#353 Wt. W3544/1454 700,000 5/15 D. D. & L. A.D.S.S./Forms/C. 2118.

SECRET.   MEDICAL.

WAR DIARY FOR MONTH OF APRIL.

74TH
FIELD AMBULANCE.
No. C 53
Date.

                              LT COL RAMC
                              O/C 74 Field Amb.

Army Form C. 2118.

WAR DIARY
or
INTELLIGENCE SUMMARY.

(Erase heading not required.)

7th FIELD AMB 2E

Page 133

Place	Date	Hour	Summary of Events and Information	Remarks and references to Appendices
Rue AMIENS 17 SAINSEN-AMIÉNOIS	1-4-18		H.Q. at TAINS. — A.D.S. at COTTENCHY. — All sick & wounded sent to 7nd F. Amb. at ST. FUSCIEN.	
—Do.—	2-4-18		—Do.— Nothing to report. Few wounded — Sick near normal. chiefly local sick.	
—Do.—	3-4-18		—Do.—	
BOVES	4-4-18		Whole unit move to BOVES & transport. Established Credit Record in Cinema. BOVES for billets for Officers and men. Number of French wounded admitted & evacuated.	
—Do.—	5-4-18		Nothing to report.	
—Do.—	6-4-18		Moved by road to SALEUX.	
SALEUX	7-4-18		Entrained at SALEUX → AMIENS → PICQUIGNY → ST. VALERY. Detrained at MOLLIÈRE (Pack ABBEVILLE. 14.) arrived MOLLIÈRE 8/4/18.	
MOLLIÈRE	8-4-18		Horse transport left BOVES 6/4/18 arrived MOLLIÈRE 8/4/18.	
—Do.—	9-4-18		Engaged in comforting backward this week, and arranging billets, cleaning clothes & all equipment. Dull weather.	
—Do.—	10-4-18		Nothing to report. Units enjoying rest, and being refitted.	
—Do.—	11-4-18		Dull weather. Route march.	
—Do.—	12-4-18		Fine weather. Route march. Visit by D.A.M.S. XVIII Corps.	
—Do.—	13-4-18		Dull weather. Worship matin v. Council. Rept'r.	
—Do.—	14-4-18		Dull weather and colder. Route march. "Yellow Birds" gave Concert in On. Rept'r. 15/4/18.	
—Do.—	15-4-18		Dull weather. Route march.	
—Do.—	16-4-18		Men confined to billets area because of infectious ent. Division cycle notes to June to 185 army Amb. — PEARES.	

Army Form C. 2118.

Page 136

WAR DIARY or INTELLIGENCE SUMMARY.

(Erase heading not required.) _In Field Ambulance_

Instructions regarding War Diaries and Intelligence Summaries are contained in F. S. Regs., Part II. and the Staff Manual respectively. Title pages will be prepared in manuscript.

Place	Date	Hour	Summary of Events and Information	Remarks and references to Appendices
MUTRIÈRE	17-4-18		Unit marched by and & Transport to WOINCOURT — arrived 11.30 p.m.	
WOINCOURT (Abbeville)	18-4-18	5 a.m.	Entrained 5 a.m. — with Coy. R.B's. — WOINCOURT → ST. POL → PERNES —	
			Arrived PERNES — marched to ORLENCOURT — billeted.	
ORLENCOURT (Lens n)	19-4-18		Resting. Foot inspection and endeavours to refitting unit & replace	
			stores — received Clerk R. Press. Cris weather. This evening Major	
Bert 38th T.B.B.			Capt. FAULKNER C.O. and CAPT. J.P. Assume temporary rank	
			of MAJOR.	
Do.	20-4-18		Unit resting.	
Do.	21-4-18		Nothing to report. O.R.M.S. conference — all O.C's F.A's Ambulance firewell. Discussion	
			regarding regarding liaison between brigades and F.A. Ambulance training relative	
			operations.	
Do.	22-4-18		Nothing to report. Divisional manoeuvre. Played drill and company drill for men.	
Do.	23-4-18		Nothing to report.	
Do.	24-4-18		Visit by G.O.C. 2nd Division, who expressed satisfaction.	
Do.	25-4-18		Capt. H. TREEN proceeds to Chapman Div. as 2.i/c 1/o 8. West Kents.	
Do.	26-4-18		Proposed site at BRYAS for D.R.S. reported by Grant railway accidents.	
Do.	27-4-18		Nothing to report. MAJOR C.J. FAULKNER interviewed by D.M.S. III Army relative to appointing	
Do.	28-4-18		for Regular Commission. S.M. RIGBY T. reported to D.R.S. on his return nor Stn. WISSANT	
Do.	29-4-18			

(Sd) R.B. Sharlin Lieut. Col., a/c D.D.

Army Form C. 2118.

Page 136.

WAR DIARY
INTELLIGENCE SUMMARY

(Erase heading not required.) 7th FIELD AMBULANCE

Place	Date	Hour	Summary of Events and Information	Remarks and references to Appendices
30-4-18 ORLENCOURT Sheet LENS. 11ᴬ			Rain - very heavy during morning. Their unit orders to move further onwards - to relieve Division in line. Which Division has had post rest and now fit for further work - battalions being kept up to strength. [signature] O.C. 7th Field Ambulance. 30/4/18	Appendix

140/2983.

No. 74 F.A.

COMMITTEE
MEDICAL HIS...
Date 9 JUL 1918

Maj. 4/8

WAR DIARY or INTELLIGENCE SUMMARY

(Erase heading not required.)

7th FIELD AMBCE

Army Form C. 2118.

Page 136

Place	Date	Hour	Summary of Events and Information	Remarks and references to Appendices
ORLENCOURT Sht/hon 1.	1-5-18		Whole unit moved from ORLENCOURT 9.30 a.m. to BEUGIN (Heu 11). Brigade formed by horse ambulance wagons.	J.F. Marsh
WERMIN (Heu 11)	2-5-18	5 p.m.	Moved to WERMIN (Heu 11) 5 p.m. Whole unit moved to GD SERVINS to take over D.R.S. from No 8 Canadian Field Ambulance.	JFM
GD SERVINS Sheet 36 B. Q.36.A.2.5.			Became Inter Brig. field. - 3 Bay, Advan Unit - Small rivers but 7 Canadian Catch. hours. - weather better.	JFM
do	3-5-18		Arranging hospital duties. - and outside work. Gas masks - weather warmer. Visited by D.D.M.S. New Cmts and rooms on roll.	JFM
do	4-5-18		Nothing to report. Work continuing.	JFM
do	5-5-18		Nothing to report. Work continuing.	JFM
do	6-5-18		R.E. Officer visited. and arranged for necessary materials for work.	JFM
do	7-5-18		Rain all day. Increased accommodation by tents, 2 Tent Subuly. - on to Chateau any one for lying cases for Scabie.	JFM
do	8-5-18		Nothing to report.	JFM
do	9-5-18		Conference took to O.C.'s Fld Amb & A.D.M.S. - Brown Division (I.O + 3268) sent up to M.D.S. - also 55 Lying Cases. Evacuated 60 lying cases to C.C.S.	JFM
do	10-5-18		Nothing to report. Work progressing. Scabies Both hours &	JFM
do	11-5-18		Nothing to report. Work progressing.	JFM

WAR DIARY
INTELLIGENCE SUMMARY.

(Erase heading not required.) **In Field**

Army Form C. 2118.

Page 137

Place	Date	Hour	Summary of Events and Information	Remarks and references to Appendices
O 3.a.7.5 Sheet 36B	12.5.18		Band of 13th Bn. R.F. played at O.R.S. from 2 pm to 6 pm.	Telegraph Wires recvd.
do.	13.5.18		Fair - but wind strong NW. Threatening rain. Some rain.	Yes
do.	14.5.18		Rifle v. Infantry "Red Diamonds" performing this afternoon. S. Sgt. Earle from Army School of Cookery reports here for 10 days him & ours.	Yes
do.	15.5.18		Divisional Band played at O.R.S. D.A.Q.M.G. Div. & XXII Corps visited this morning to see accommodation.	Yes
do.	16.5.18		Major Eayrie and another Div. Instructor proceeded to take over Ambulance HQ at ESTRÉE CAUCHIE with a view to establish Corps Mini P.	Yes
do.	17.5.18		Nothing to report. V. warm and fine weather.	Yes
do.	18.5.18		Fine warm weather continues.	Yes
do.	19.5.18		Band of 3rd R.F.'s performed afternoon and evening.	Yes
do.	20.5.18		"Red Diamonds" gave a show here. Fine warm weather.	Yes
do.	21.5.18		Strong winds - and indeed all Corps troops remaining to be engaged.	Yes
do.	22.5.18		Surgeon (an Instructor here to be looked at) open air stops. Fine weather.	Yes
do.	23.5.18		V. high wind - "Yellow Book" love & guns to forward.	Yes

Army Form C. 2118.

WAR DIARY
or
INTELLIGENCE SUMMARY.

(Erase heading not required.) 7th FIELD AMBULANCE.

Page 138

Place	Date	Hour	Summary of Events and Information	Remarks and references to Appendices
O3 c. a. 7.5. West 36d	24-5-18		Revise all day. Nil. Band played in woods in afternoon.	Germaith Mars
Do	25-5-18		Notes Coys. rec. Cadre. R.E. work progressing but considerable amount yet to be completed.	pt
Do	26-5-18		Band 7.15 in evening. Sergt. Lankoski took specials to 1st Army School of Cookery after 16 days Cmn 2 night.	pt
Do	27-5-18		Nothing to report. 14 & 15th Canadian Cav. Band postponed.	pt
Do	28-5-18		Pte. Ricketts filling unit Dentures for crowns of Molars 1st Army Dental School.	pt
Do	29-5-18		Pte. Strickland A.S.C. M.T. attached to unit as M.T. Eng.	pt
Do	30-5-18		Bn of 116th Division N.C.O. Instructors at this DRS.	pt
Do	31-5-18		Cinema show to patients. Films been machine. Patients remaining at DRS on last day of month 161. Admissions chiefly Pyrexia. Birds other than men Flu epidemic. Interclean Carriers 4. Rose m's a. 4. Diphtheria 1. Suppuration 1.	pt

Edward Mars
[signature]

16/3076

June 1918

Army Form C. 2118.

Page 13?

WAR DIARY
INTELLIGENCE SUMMARY
(Erase heading not required.)

7th E. FIELD AMBULANCE

Place	Date	Hour	Summary of Events and Information	Remarks and references to Appendices
O 34 c 9.5 Brut Wd B.	1-6-18		Three were malaria. Qr. Master reports food & water — no course of outbreak. 15th army Rural School.	Appendix Titles
Do	2-6-18		Continuation of fine weather.	
Do	3-6-18		46th Canadian Band gave entertainment in hospital grounds.	
Do	4-6-18		"Red Diamonds" gave concert to patients.	
Do	5-6-18		Band of 9th E. Surreys perform. Fine weather.	
Do	6-6-18		Fine weather continues. MOs to inspect Corps Rest Camp. Assist in process of evacuation.	
Do	7-6-18		Delay due to lack of RE material — transportation. Motors to inspect. Ball and awl.	
Do	8-6-18		MOs to inspect.	
Do	9-6-18		Band of 46th Bn. Canadians played in this DRS.	
Do	10-6-18		MOs to inspect. "D" division inspect "Delousen" at Corps Rest Camp.	
Do	11-6-18		2nd Div. Band (French).	
Do	12-6-18		Red Diamonds Concert Party. Fair performance of patients.	
Do	13-6-18		D. and C. Corps visits. General chaos causing of outbreak now Lt E "Mayg?" — absent epidemic. (Diarrhoea complicated in patns. Diarrhoea patns on Table #3).	

WAR DIARY
INTELLIGENCE SUMMARY

Army Form C. 2118.

Page 140.

No. 1 F.F.L.D M.R.S.F.

Place	Date	Hour	Summary of Events and Information	Remarks and references to Appendices
D'Zuares Short 62B	14-6-18		Ambulance open for "Infective Pyrexia" contacts. 7 Sitting cases & 8 patient accommodation.	[illegible sig]
Do	15-6-18		Nothing of interest to report.	
Do	16-6-18		Slack day. New cases of I.P. found by their afternoon. 4 unsuspected. These were apparently all in patients.	
Do	17-6-18		66 cases Infective Pyrexia in D.R.S. including 18 O.R. among this unit. Recovery quick and apparently complete.	
Do	18-6-18		Many of the Canadian R.E. patients. Heavy rain in afternoon and evening.	
Do	19-6-18		96 cases of Infective Pyrexia remaining. 196 cases of "Infective Pyrexia" remaining — including 21 of this unit, 1 O.R. transport, 71 cases Pyjia sick to Corps Rest Camp. Into & release carrying hand. Capt McDonald came through to Entuary D.G. ule 73rd F.A. Total 378 in hospital - (including 21 O.R. of this unit & Pyrexia out of 262 cases) commence to dis-D "delousing" adjacent to Batt. h.q. maps.	
Do	20-6-18			
Do	21-6-18		Total 296 Pyrexia cases remaining - Sans Mis 412. Hole market. Some rain.	
Do	22-6-18		Total 269 Pyrexia cases remaining 165. heavier thunder—high wind.	
Do	23-6-18		Nothing to report. Daily Pyrexia report sent although from Depot.	
Do	24-6-18		left Capt Buttigs relieved by Capt McMasters & Entuary D.G. 5 J.E. Emery 15.	

WAR DIARY

INTELLIGENCE SUMMARY

7th Field Ambulance.

Place	Date	Hour	Summary of Events and Information	Remarks
Q 34.a 25	25-6-18		Capt H.S. Pugh. Junior Surgeon. 1 OR admitted here for H.S. Col. End of month. Board of Comdts. sitting (no Pres) played in camp. Injured weather.	[sig]
Do	26-6-18		Nothing to report.	[sig]
Do	27-6-18		Band of 11th Res. REGT.O played in his DRS. fine weather. Nothing to report.	[sig]
Do	28-6-18		Continuation of this match. Nothing to report.	[sig]
Do	29-6-18		Nothing to report.	[sig]
Do	30-6-18		S. Major R/17 admitted from here. This month has been notorious because of the increased number of 2 & 3 day Pyrexia. Sudden onset. 5 malaria. Headache. Pains in eyes. epididymitis. pharyngitis. Temp 101-103°. lethargy. lupus. afterwards low. (some recurrence of temp). Debility, anaemia, etc. notes.) Most infection carried by presence? Total men here admitted this Dec beginning myo Pyrexia for month = 817	[sig]

[signatures]

140/2131.

No. 747.a.

July 1918

24

Army Form C. 2118.

WAR DIARY
or
INTELLIGENCE SUMMARY.

(Erase heading not required.) 7th FIELD AMBULANCE.

Instructions regarding War Diaries and Intelligence Summaries are contained in F. S. Regs., Part II. and the Staff Manual respectively. Title pages will be prepared in manuscript.

Place	Date	Hour	Summary of Events and Information	Remarks and references to Appendices
O.34.c.2.5. Ster 4e*	1-7-18		Band of D.C.C. 70 Dist. played in Dec. Fine warm weather.	
″	2-7-18		Continued fine warm weather.	
″	3-7-18		Band of 70th Div. played in D.R.S.	
″	4-7-18		Our Picture complete and ready for use.	
″	5-7-18		Nothing to report.	
″	6-7-18		Padre Empl. "Shepper" and Miss Beaver performed at the O.R.S. S.S. Sunders visits. Great performance.	
″	7-7-18		Nothing to report.	
″	8-7-18		Band of 9th Sunwood. played in camp. 11 casualties (not serious) 2 killed from bomb wounds 1 am. 1 Lieut. Botkin M.O.R.C. 0.54 returns to his dept. Capt. MacDonnell came attends from due to 1st Rey. Fuse air. and in leave.	
″	9-7-18		"It Ginsberg M.O.R.C. 0.54 & parts for Paler "Yellow Brick" (are shown in Kinnetts Row.	
″	10-7-18		Red Diamonds performed. 147 mens and some rain.	

A7091. Wt. W12839/M1292. 750,000. 1/17. D, D & L., Ltd. Forms/C2118/14.

Army Form C. 2118.

Sheet No 3

WAR DIARY
or
INTELLIGENCE SUMMARY.

(Erase heading not required.) In FIELD MARSEILLES

Place	Date	Hour	Summary of Events and Information	Remarks and references to Appendices
Q.3a, c, 25 SKELLHUB	11-7-18		Band and train Making transport.	
Do.	12-7-18		Band 9 & 10 Mid. played in Camp. Guard 2024 R.S.M & his NCO on Orderly Duties. Inspection and kit 15 by Brigadier for troops from Peter. G.H.Q.	
Do.	13-7-18		Nothing to report.	
Do.	14-7-18		Warrant ordr hdr Coffee Mr Cards is put to be handed on to an Ambulance of 52nd Division.	
Do.	15-7-18		Thunderstorm & heavy rain at night. Inhabitants in apprehensive of further storms.	
Do.	16-7-18		Pte Brown and (Pte Shaw) in Brandon Room after Div Court Martial on to Field Ambulance. Very warm weather.	
Do.	17-7-18		Continuation program walking kindr, bythming n heavy rain. Returnd to 3rd K.Rifles, performed in tour D&E.	
Do.	18-7-18		Nothing to report.	
Do.	19-7-18		Visit 72nd, 73rd Field Ambulances - fine warm weather.	
Do.	20-7-18		Thunderstorms and rain - fine intervals. Yellow Robi performed.	
Do.	21-7-18		The Band played in afternoon. Strong wind - hazier. Nice cool weather from Army RAF Camp.	

Army Form C. 2118.

Sheet 744.

WAR DIARY
INTELLIGENCE SUMMARY
7th FIELD AMBULANCE
(Erase heading not required.)

Instructions regarding War Diaries and Intelligence Summaries are contained in F. S. Regs., Part II, and the Staff Manual respectively. Title pages will be prepared in manuscript.

Place	Date	Hour	Summary of Events and Information	Remarks and references to Appendices
O.3.a. & m.7.a.B. Shot Wd B.	22.7.18		Band 97th D.C.L.I. (20th Div.) played at O.R.S. Red Diamonds performed here. Heavy rain. Band in Camp	Appendix
Do-	23.7.18		visits to See Division —	Yes
Do-	24.7.18		Nil entries — Entr of 7th F.A. hereafter Rgt. performed here.	Appx A
Do-			Private walks —	
Do-	25.7.18		20th Div. Band played at O.R.S. Capt. A.M. MacDonald returns to this unit. Two autographs on neg. 16 1st Bn. R. Fusiliers	Appx
Do-	26.7.18		27. P.A. MANSFIELD once refused to be for any duty. Admits visits Camp. PTE. T. J.P. STUART once this unit. refused to 17 Inf. Bn. for 1 month. Allotment to an infantry Bn. not a nice to conunsion —	Appx
Do-	27.7.18		A change to report. Heavy rain accident.	Yes
Do-	28.7.18		Band 17 Bn N.F. played in Camp.	Ditto
Do-	29.7.18		A change to report. From warm day. Shot Laren evacuates to 7th F.A. under fine weather. Medicines for events to obtain more accommodation for the ORs.	Yes
Do-	30.7.18		Fine weather. Medicine for events to obtain more accommodation [added]	Yes
Do-	31.7.18		Fine warm weather. Commander Colonel's warn -	Appendix

WA 35
140/3200

19
Aug. 1918

Confidential

War Diary
of
74th Field Ambulance

From :- 1/8/1918   To. 31st/8/1918.

Army Form C. 2118.

Page 145.

WAR DIARY
INTELLIGENCE SUMMARY.
(Erase heading not required.) 7th FIELD AMB.

Place	Date	Hour	Summary of Events and Information	Remarks and references to Appendices
Azuara est. Studios	1-8-18		Fine warm weather. Events (Field hat being continued) The following more into June -	
Do.	2-8-18		Capt. Cuy. M.R. has went to Pts Auccons - Capt. MacDonald. Comp. has went to 1/2 N. Staff. Capt. Rethie returned to this unit for temporary duty on No. 1st N. Staff. Capt. Cond. C.N. Roume reported for duty - for final re-Enlistment (31-7-18) from training Brigade.	
Do.	3-8-18		E.O.R. paraded to their tent for Parade. Events many series of cricket & 32nd Reg'l. played in camp. Tent webs received 9.10 P.m. Thunderstorm followed - 1 Brown Public. paraded to M.D.S. returned from myst. (Rain) Yeoman B.S.B. from then at D.R.C.	
Do.	4-8-18		Anniversary of 4th Year of war. Commemoration Service held at Army H.Q. 1 Man. W.O.R. this morl. alone.	
Do.	5-8-18		Band & 11th R. Ref. Regl. played in camp. Rain - Work & training hitherto continued.	
Do.	6-8-18		Capt. C.N. Coad. W.C. Roume reported for duty - taken on strength from 31-7-18. O.R.E. visited & roume. Two pages to hosp.	
Do.	7-8-18		Nothing to report.	
Do.	8-8-18		Fine hot weather - Nothing to report.	

Army Form C. 2118.

WAR DIARY
or
INTELLIGENCE SUMMARY.
(Erase heading not required.)

74th Field Ambulance   Page 146

Place	Date	Hour	Summary of Events and Information	Remarks and references to Appendices
Q 36.a 25. Sheet 44.C	9-8-18		Divisional Horse Show - Our unit won 1st prize RAMC Turn out (wheeled and Ambulance type.) "Yellow Bird" 1st prize show at O.R.S.	J Broomfield Lieut
Do	10-8-18		Band of R.G.A. Sinings played in camp. Won 2 hot contested contures. No rain. Band played in afternoon. Some malaria.	Do
Do	11-8-18			Do
Do	12-8-18		Sgt T. Williams killed. Our unit required to give Bearers & Officer - Rain till evening attack. No rain wrestler.	Do
Do	13-8-18		Band of 115 Mahrattas played in camp. No Bugn - Myr Concert Party (73rd/13th) performed at 5.30	Do
Do	14-8-18		Band of 8th Northumberland Fus. played in camp. Some malaria - WEPID Lieut E of 15 Army will inspect this station 10am 16th inst.	Do
Do	15-8-18		Nothing to report. Some malaria continues.	Do
Do	16-8-18		Inspected by D.D.M.S. 15 Army - who expressed which satisfaction with personnel and work of others. No special reports.	Do
Do	17-8-18		Quite day. calm. No event and rather 73°F Pte Amba. on visit - 94F	Do
Do	18-8-18		Band of 8th Durh. played in camp. Cricket match v Dir Head qrs.	Do
Do	19-8-18		Visits of RAMC and MO.B to Marswa front both arrived to taking this in No. 5.	Do
Do	20-8-18		Showers of rain. Unit to rest and most in relief of personnel & 72nd Fd Ambc	Do

Army Form C. 2118.

WAR DIARY
of
INTELLIGENCE SUMMARY.
(Erase heading not required.)

Instructions regarding War Diaries and Intelligence Summaries are contained in F.S. Regs., Part II. and the Staff Manual respectively. Title pages will be prepared in manuscript.

4th Field Ambulance   page 147

Place	Date	Hour	Summary of Events and Information	Remarks and references to Appendices
R.8.C. Shot.w.B	21/8/18		The DRS at Q.34.a.2.5. Shot.w.B. handed over to 93rd Field Ambulance. The MDS at R.8.C. Shot.w.B. taken over from the Field Amb. to be emptied by 6 pm 21/8/18. ADMS notified later on. Posts employed Lt Col J.C. Davison proceeded on leave the date duties taken over by Major C.P. Walker R.A.M.C. Lt H Bothin A.R.C. U.S.A. returned from Ypres Aug 5th. 242' A.F.A.	O.M. Davison Major
Do	22/8/18		The villages in heavy shell fire from 6 H.m. to 8 p/o midnight - several civilian casualties it is not known to an Dressing & S.P. Post.	O.T.
Do	23/8/18		Visited both ADS: and all dressing posts. Anything unusual. Materials set. Sorel G. MaGr and Yosh Posts in the Bn area 1 equipment. Got to have this day - the men formed to have during the night to civilian casualties.	O.L
Do	24/8/18		The main dressing station was inspected by the ADMS this morning - the same instructions to have block C strengthened.	A.L

Army Form C. 2118.

WAR DIARY
of 7th Field Ambulance

INTELLIGENCE SUMMARY.
(Erase heading not required.)

Instructions regarding War Diaries and Intelligence
Summaries are contained in F. S. Regs., Part II.
and the Staff Manual respectively. Title pages
will be prepared in manuscript.

Place	Date	Hour	Summary of Events and Information	Remarks and references to Appendices
Sheet 44B R.8 Central	25/9/18		Major C.S Fowler was evacuated to No 2 2 CCS to-day - the acting command of the unit was taken over by Major J. P. Collin.	Appendix Major
	26/9/18		Visited Fort Blair to-day with D.A D.M.S.	do
	27/9/18		The M.D.S was inspected to-day by the G.O.C 8th Corps. Fort Blair was handed over to 45th Field Ambulance this evening. All R.A.M.C personnel on the left bivouac Sector were withdrawn Co. H.Q. The Post at Marne is still maintained	do
	28/9/18		Nothing unusual to report	do
	29/9/18		Capt R. J. Duthie & 18 O.R.S were relieved at A.D.S St Pierre to-day by Capt R.C Lowe & 18 O.R.S	do
	30.9.18		Rejoined from Paris leave. 2 days before rejoining to leave.	[signature] Lieut RAMC
	31.9.18		Nothing to report. [signature] Lieut RAMC O.C 7th Fd. Amb. 3/9/18.	do

160/3259.

W.F. Amb.

Sept-Oct 1918.

COMMITTEE FOR
MEDICAL HISTORY
Date 9 NOV 1918

Army Form C. 2118.

WAR DIARY
or
INTELLIGENCE SUMMARY.
(Erase heading not required.) 7th (Field) Ambulance

Place	Date	Hour	Summary of Events and Information	Remarks and references to Appendices
P.B. Centre Mustan Rd.	1-9-18		Visited A.D.S. and R.A.P.s and med. comforts no. Teuckin - also on Jerusalem Road accompanied. Fine weather.	Appendix two
Do	2-9-18		Fine weather. Took on what W.W.C.P. and P.O.W. at FOSSE 2: fm 72nd F.A.	App 2a
Do	3-9-18		R.A.M.S. visited M.D.S. Pay paid.	App 2b & and ST. PIERRE.
Do	4-9-18		also Valley P.O.W. Few malaria. Visited cases of "Spanish" meningitis v/w real or clinical. Nothing to report. Spraying.	App 2c
Do - 5-9-18			Visited A.D.Ss and R.A.P. (Valley PoP) - Saw some cases of Laryngitis - delayed follow t. 7 to 10 days after exposure. Orders cases to remain at duty except those c hyperemia.	App 2d
Do - 6-9-18			Fine weather. Over 50 (?) cases admitted and evacuated - mostly Yellow F. and (?) carpentering, white-washing and something. No beams.	App 2e
Do - 7-9-18			Contracts of fine weather. Remonstrate of lives of unstable persons in water.	App 2f
Do - 8-9-18			Nothing to report.	App 2g
Do - 9-9-18			Visited M.D.S. & W.W.C.P. FOSSE 2: - Damage done by one being multiplied - repairs to latrines - new fitting hut. Cold being being constructed.	App 2h
Do - 10-9-18			Nothing to report. Less malaria - curve.	App 2i
Do - 11-9-18			Visited A.D.S. and W.W.C.P. - hyperemia disappeared at A.D.S.	App 2j

Page 145

No. 36

Army Form C. 2118.

WAR DIARY
of
INTELLIGENCE SUMMARY.
(Erase heading not required.)

No Fire Ambulance Page 150

Place	Date	Hour	Summary of Events and Information	Remarks and references to Appendices
R.S. Curles (W.A.)	12-9-18		Allied conference at HQMD this 10-12.30. het matter continue.	
	13-9-18		Visits R.A.P.s & W.W.C.P. - R.A.P.'s begun on with analysis instantly. Lost for previous 2 & 2.65 ft. Nothing to report.	
	14-9-18			
	15-9-18		Magr. Conn returns for leave this P.M. Visits Fwd D. W.W.C.P.	
	16-9-18		Visits valley R.A.P. - men taken in by 7nd Fd. Amb. Convoy wounded. Visits Fwd D. W.W.C.P. - practice been at 2.31 p.m. of walking wounded.	
	17-9-18		Visits Fwd D. R.A.S. and new R.A.P.S.	
	18-9-18		Visits Fwd. Line, but a visit to entire of evacuation forwards from new R.A.P.S. Cheapside evacn - some rain. About visits to "diantico carts".	
	19-9-18			
	20-9-18		Few ha cases admitted. 7 Blue eum. Nothing to report.	
	21-9-18		Visits R.A.P.s and R.A.P.'s. Rain in afternoon.	
	22-9-18		Agins visits HQMD - examined him u officials of Nerves Splint.	
	23-9-18		Conference HQMD this re morn. Subject intensifying of col division. Nothing to report. Corps Command. hands pay to officers of Division.	
	24-9-18		HQ. R.A.M.C. - Judge for Short recent of limit.	
	25-9-18			
	26-9-18		Professional . . . kind being carried out.	

WAR DIARY
or
INTELLIGENCE SUMMARY.

(Erase heading not required.) 96 FIELD AMBULANCE. Page 157.

Army Form C. 2118.

Place	Date	Hour	Summary of Events and Information	Remarks and references to Appendices
R.E. Dump (44°)	27-9-18		Fine weather. Officers from B/1 and C/2 tendered Mme Cavalie Fd. Amb. visited M.D.S. preparatory to reading advance parties to B/1 and D for taking over.	
Do.	28-9-18		D.D.M.S. VIII Corps visited [illeg] Parents.	
Do.	29-9-18		Advance parties for B/1, Mme Cavalie Fd. Amb. arrived & took over [illeg]. ... D/2 Mme Cavalie Fd Amb. arrived & took over M.D.S.	
Do.	30-9-18		Stayed at MERSIN to night 30/1. — offrs handing over to B/1 and D/2 96th Field Ambulances. 17. MANSFIELD & ROME transferred to D/2 Field Ambulance.	

[signature]
Major R.A.M.C.
O.C. 96 Field Ambulance.

Oct 1918

M.O/3324

Jack F. Andre

Army Form C.-2118.

WAR DIARY
of
INTELLIGENCE SUMMARY.
(Erase heading not required.) 1/4 FIELD AMBULANCE.

Page 150

Place	Date	Hour	Summary of Events and Information	Remarks and references to Appendices
IVERGNY. 57.C. Sheet (N.W.)	1-10-18		Entered WAR and BOUQUEMAISON — marched to IVERGNY — arrived 5:30 p.m. Huts and M.T. transport by road. Fine weather — Battle font. Wounded accommodated 1 Division Scale. Horse standings for	[signatures]
—Do.—	2-10-18		Settling down in billets. Cleaning up ground which was found to front of huts. Training programme arranged & commence tomorrow. Rest & march.	
—Do.—	3-10-18		Commenced training. Personnel being rested. 7½ hours intensive day. Fine weather. Continued training.	
—Do.—	4-10-18			
—Do.—	5-10-18		Major Cain left & transport by road — staying at BOIRY for night. Training finished.	
—Do.—	6-10-18		Entrained at BOUQUEMAISON — detrained at WARINCOURT — marched to GRAINCOURT.	
GRAINCOURT (Sheet 57.E.)	7-10-18		Arrived GRAINCOURT. Bivouac. Moved to ANNEUX night 7/8.	
ANNEUX —Do.—	8-10-18		in tents and bivouacs —	
NIERGNIES.	9-10-18		Moved to NIERGNIES and established M.D.S. at ECHU — opening 2200 hours. Saveur & Duke	
—Do.—	10-10-18		Working M.D.S.	
—Do.—	11-10-18		Moved to W. of AVESNES-LES-AUBERS — passing on fires & transport. Returned to A.D.S. 73 Fd. Ambce. Same night. (Success at B.B.B.?)	
MESSAGES 12-10-18 AUBERS			Established A.D.S. in ex German hospital — few casualties. Slightly damaged by electricity.	
	13-10-18		Nothing to report. Very few wounds being evacuated.	

WAR DIARY of INTELLIGENCE SUMMARY

Army Form C. 2118.

(Erase heading not required.) 7/4 FIELD AMBULANCE

App 157

Place	Date	Hour	Summary of Events and Information	Remarks and references to Appendices
MESNIERES-MESNERS.	13-10-18		V. busy. Many wounded cases. Had nos. 2. 8, 3, 84 Divisions. Non-arrival forced 3 cases moving to C.C. S. rest to reserves.	J. E. March Lieut
Do.	14-10-18		Non busy.	App.
Do.	15-10-18		Quiet. Also 250 civilian evacuees from HAUSSY & AVESNES.	Jet
Do.	16-10-18		Busy. Allies 6, 7" D's 1.8. - 250 cases chans to Rebais.	Jet.
CAGNONCLES	17-10-18		57 F/A under 19th Div. relieved. Their rear party marched to CAGNONCLES.	App.
Do.	18-10-18		Engaged in clearing up billets. Re-equipping personnel.	App
(6.4.A. 9.E.) Sheet 57B.	19-10-18		Brigd Ghark Commenced. This unit v. 3rd R. 13's at breen - Left 7.0.1. Relieved by 7/2 Cork Mustans F.A. (61st Div.) and marched to 63vis as Faubourg de Droven.	App.
CAMBRAI. [Fau. ST DENON]	20-10-18		Settling down to billets. Lost mules. Baths per hot-sections - all beran under cover.	App.
Do -	21-10-18		Continuation of damp weather. Commandant of training. Spent air Ferblanc being attached to Hay. nashy and arrived training.	App.
Do -	22-10-18		Wet weather. G.O.C. 2th Div. visited and conveyed thanks to God work of R.A.M.C. Sw. cleared much active practice.	Les
Do.	23-10-18		Fine weather. Continuation of training - special trainfram & Qualking - and thank her for Brigd Final. proceeded an leave Ground - leaving U.F. MAJOR. T.R. CAMIR. R.A.M.C.	J.E. March Lieut

14

WAR DIARY
or
INTELLIGENCE SUMMARY.

(Erase heading not required.)

Army Form C. 2118.

72 Field Amb. R.A.M.C. Vol 3 Page 14.

Place	Date	Hour	Summary of Events and Information	Remarks and references to Appendices
OMBREM [Fm. St. Druon]	24-10-18		Capt. L. H Taylor RAMC T.C was posted to "72nd Field Ambulance today. Weather continues fine.	J.F. Cohen Major
CAGNONCLES B4,a,28 (57B)	25-10-18		Unit moved to Cagnoncles this morning and took up former billets. 1st Lieut J.R Campbell M.O.T.C. was attached to duty for temporary duty.	JFC
St Aubert R.15.d.99 (51 A)	26-10-18		Unit moved into St Aubert to-day. Billets scattered. Weather fine.	JFC
do	27-10-18		Nothing to report. 1st Lieut Campbell was posted to 8th F. w Hants for temporary duty.	JFC
do	28-10-18		Nothing to report.	JFC
do	29-10-18		Nothing to report	JFC
do	30-10-18		Nothing to rep ort	JFC
	31-10-18		Capt Macdonald F.B was attached to this unit to-day for temporary duty.	JFC

J F Cohen
Major RAMC

149/3401

14.7.a.

Nov 1918

COMMITTEE FOR THE
MEDICAL HISTORY OF THE WAR
Date 20 JAN 1919

Army Form C. 2118.

WAR DIARY
INTELLIGENCE SUMMARY

(Erase heading not required.)

7th FIELD AMBULANCE   Page 163

Place	Date	Hour	Summary of Events and Information	Remarks and references to Appendices
St Aubert A.18 a 9.9 (51A)	1/11/18		Warning order received to-day to be prepared to move with the 17th I.B. Weather rather cold. rain showers	JF
St Aubert V.13 c 5.5	2/11/18		Unit side slipped with regard to billets this morning – Close billetting has had to be done. Weather dull & showery	JF
Bermerain 3/11/18 Q.22 a.4.4 (51A)	3/11/18		Unit marched off this morning at 4 a.m & arrived here at 7 A.M. Runners were posted @ 17 I.B. B.H.Q & bearers with the three battalions in the Brigade.	JF
Jenlain L.23 c.5.9 Sheet 51A	4/11/18		Unit marched in here & form an A.D.S. rather severe hostile shelling for about 30 minutes after our arrival. Many casualties amongst 1st Battalion Royal Fusiliers and 2 casualties amongst personnel of Ambulance (Pte Petty & Penny)	JF
Warnies le Petit G.34 a.5.9 Sheet 51	5/11/18		Unit moved to here & formed an A.D.S. in the Chateau. Capt Coad & 3 bearers (Pte Drope, McCarthy & Brown) were wounded to-day. Pte Whick, Driver Benwyer were gassed (shell) all were evacuated. 3 M.O's from 72nd Field Ambulance came to assist as duty a few minutes. Casualties were dealt with. Capt Suther assumed the duties of second Officer – weather very wet	JF
do	6/11/18			JF

Army Form C. 2118.

WAR DIARY
INTELLIGENCE SUMMARY.
(Erase heading not required.)

In FIELD AMBULANCE

Page 154

Instructions regarding War Diaries and Intelligence Summaries are contained in F. S. Regs., Part II. and the Staff Manual respectively. Title pages will be prepared in manuscript.

Place	Date	Hour	Summary of Events and Information	Remarks and references to Appendices
Warnies to Petit G34a5-9 Sheet 51	7/11/18		Unit is working the A.D.S. here – weather very wet – a fair number of casualties have been dealt with	Howein' hours'
BAVAY G25a90 Sheet 51	8/11/18		Unit moved to-day to new billets – bearers returned from 17 I.B. weather very damp.	do.
do	9/11/18		Nothing to report	do
do	10/11/18		A bearing party of 1 Sgt + 19 O.R.'s were posted this evening at the German Hospital in the Rue de Mons – weather crew of me	do.
do	11/11/18		Copy of message received from H.Q. 17.I.B. "Hostilities will cease at 11.00 hours to-day November 11th. Troops will stand fast on the line reached by that hour which will be communicated to Divisional H.Q. by wire. Defensive precautions will be maintained. There will be no intercourse of any description with the enemy." Ronald M Scotrid Captain Brigade Major 17th Infantry Brigade	

11th November 1918.

Army Form C. 2118.

WAR DIARY
INTELLIGENCE SUMMARY.
7th Field Ambulance Page 155.

(Erase heading not required.)

Place	Date	Hour	Summary of Events and Information	Remarks and references to Appendices
BAVAY J.25.a.9.0. Sheet 51.	11/11/18		A reinforcement of 8 Privates arrived to-day. Lieut. Col. F.C.D. Bircher resumed command of the Unit	
do.	12/11/18		Received Command Fruit. Nothing to report. Billets comfortable. Plenty Canteen supplies.	
do.	13/11/18		Nothing to report. Jan. nealin. anti-Snr.	
do.	14/11/18		Thanksgiving service held at Bavai under RC Chap. arrangement. Please attend this service=75.	
do.	15/11/18		Cape Pallis departs on leave. Capt. Taylor RAMC returned to 72nd Fd Auntie. Warning order received that no Fd R.R. will move 185th to 7th Army Ave.	
do.	16/11/18		Rest - Jan. nealin. Hauled in 1 H.Q. Amer to Fd Cmft. Canteens are now authorized.	
JENLAIN 17/11/18 Valenciennes 1.100.000			Rec'd w/o Brigade prop for Bavai to JENLAIN. R Whts and Stones. Fine.	
OISY	18/11/18		Rec'd w/o Brigade Sumf to OISY. B.Whts good. Fine. Some snow.	
do.				
SOMAIN	19/11/18		Rec'd w/o Brigade Sumf. Weather Chch.	

WAR DIARY or INTELLIGENCE SUMMARY

Army Form C. 2118.

74

(Erase heading not required.) The FIELD AMBULANCE.

Page 158

Place	Date	Hour	Summary of Events and Information	Remarks and references to Appendices
SOMAIN (Valenciennes 1-100,000)	20-11-18.		Units mobilized weather. Attended meeting at B.H.Q. re demobilization. Arranging for talks for inspection many old German installations in training, all open to view.	Illegible
—do—	21-11-18.		Nothing to report.	—
—do—	22-11-18.		Meeting of Board of Central of Venereal lectures given — Lt appoints President. Warning noticed warning the Brigade area to TOURNAI area on or about 25.5. For body mobile.	Illegible
—do—	23-11-18.		Nothing to report. Nurses released to R.A.F. 3rd relief — 22 nurses (free nurses) in this unit.	Illegible
—do—	24-11-18.		Nothing to report.	Illegible
—do—	25-11-18.		Nothing to report.	Illegible
RUMEGIES (Valenciennes 1-100,000)	26-11-18. 27-11-18.		Moved with Brigade Group to RUMEGIES — Billets poor. Nothing to report.	Illegible
—do—	28-11-18.		Capt BARKER proceeded to D.R.S. à 71 Labour Group — Chief of Staff — Lt WELLER wrote via Billets in strength. (W. of Journal)	Illegible
—do—	29-11-18.		Nothing to report. Proposed new area at BRISON.	—
—do—	30-11-18.		Moved with 7th Inf. Bde. Group to BRISON — whole village billets to this unit. Billets not very poor — no latrines — cookhouses. Hospital and H.Q. established in Chateau.	Illegible

No. 74 F. U.

COMMITTEE FOR THE
MEDICAL HISTORY OF THE WAR
6 MAR 1919
Date

WAR DIARY or INTELLIGENCE SUMMARY

Army Form C. 2118.

(Erase heading not required.) 76 FIELD AMBULANCE

Place	Date	Hour	Summary of Events and Information	Remarks and references to Appendices
GOUSON (Sheet 27) 1-10000	1-12-18		Settling down in new billets. General cleaning up.	Werner Weiss RAMC
Do	2-12-18		Nothing to report.	
Do	3-12-18		A.D.M.S. visited and inspected Unit. O.C. held conference of Officers. Fine day. Rough weather.	
Do	4-12-18		Inspection of billets.	
Do	5-12-18		Continuation of above inspection. Unit needing to discuss terms for billets.	
Do	6-12-18		Nothing to report.	
Do	7-12-18		Hon. King James from TOURAI-LILLE road 7.30 p.m. Detachment 2 men from brigade interviewed in road.	
Do	8-12-18		Nothing to report. Church Parade (13 C.C.S.) & allowed Parade, Sundays, Monday, Tuesday weekly. Commencing from this date.	
Do	9-12-18		Nothing to report. Employed in various conditions.	
Do	10-12-18		Do. Arrival of first Consignment of beer - much welcomed. Latrines, baths and their sanitary appearance obtained for hospital - 6 beds &c.	
Do	11-12-18		Nurses applied for demobilization. First batch to report 13th inst.	
Do	12-12-18		Rain. Nothing to report.	
Do	13-12-18		Bathes for personnel complete and opened this date for daily use.	
Do	14-12-18		Nothing to report. Leave bath 2 nurses sent to England - no Warrant Officer.	
Do	15-12-18		Dull weather.	

WAR DIARY
INTELLIGENCE SUMMARY

(Erase heading not required.) 7th FIELD AMBULANCE

Army Form C. 2118.

Page 15F

Place	Date	Hour	Summary of Events and Information	Remarks and references to Appendices
GOUZON (Sheet 33) (1-10000) M.13.central.	16-12-18		Nothing to report. Very fine bright weather. Duties: Preparing winter quarters for billeting to Township Lodg. of this unit.	
Do	17-12-18		Nothing to report.	
Do	18-12-18		155 Coy. A.T.C. who have been trenches in this village moved to PETERMAN, leaving vacant the 17th Bn. Welsh (R.E.) Company ville be occupying 67x16 in lieu etc. in a few days. This (Strength - Officer 3, men 100) Nothing to report. Tent division shiftes to dug-out etc.	
Do	19-12-18			
Do	20-12-18		A.F. 2/16 received. Sent out and received on Major T.R.CARTER returns from leave to PARIS 16/12 to 21/12/18.	
Do	21-12-18		Nothing further.	
Do	22-12-18		Gaoling to report. Much rain, whole pass under from to Lourd and a heavy Nothing to Round and Ladi. New Frank st clop. R.S.M.	
Do	23-12-18			
Do	24-12-18		Visit of Lut fut N.A. - Fortress medals in afternoon. Personal service at night. Few made.	
Do	25-12-18		Fine weather.	
Do	26-12-18		Rain all day. Last batch of winter draftees to England for disposal leaving in them unit.	
Do	27-12-18			
Do	28-12-18		B.S.I. f 30 for this unit.	
Do	29-12-18		Nothing to report.	
Do	30-12-18		Showery weather - much rain.	
Do	31-12-18		For orderly LT. WELLS has been ordered to 30 E.C.R.S.	

31/12/18 O.C. 9th Aust...

24 DIV   Box 1952

No 74 Field Ambulance

Army Form C. 2118

WAR DIARY
or
INTELLIGENCE SUMMARY. 7th FIELD AMBCE
(Erase heading not required.)

Page 135

Place	Date	Hour	Summary of Events and Information	Remarks and references to Appendices
GRUGIES (Abt 37 C.W.)	1-1-19		Conference at A.D.M.S Office - to discuss plan of demobilization - postal schedules & routine	
(Nr 33 C.C.S.)	2-1-19		LT. HELLER. M.O.R.C. U.S.A retired from here to England - 5 days return rail & visit H.Q. Prior to	
Do	3-1-19		London. Nothing to report.	
Do	4-1-19		Made trip to 7(?) Field Ambulance units. Visit 521. Ground almost unplayable owing to recent rain D.	
Do	5-1-19		CAPT R.L. ANDREW R.A.M.C. reports for duty. From 84th Divisn - Taken on strength, pleas units via S.O.E	
Do	6-1-19		Fine weather. News of CAPT. ANDREW announced and marched.	
Do	7-1-19		Lecture given 3 p.m. by Mr. Macaughlin - Announcin Stn. Engr - on "Cattles & Kalli"	
Do	8-1-19		Major J.P. CAMP. R.A.M.C. (E. Englan) in establishin Officers Commission -	
Do	9-1-19		Owing his station visits from Paris & ratifies rule emergency case. Heavy rain.	
Do	10-1-19		Nothing to report.	
Do	11-1-19		Accounts & I follows for Demobilizati on U.S.	
Do	12-1-19		Interview with Div Comand at D.M.S. on Canteen Board. Nothing to report.	
Do	13-1-19		Allied General Camp mates at 17 NOTERN HQ. 11 am. Take forwards & towards to see	
Do	14-1-19		Div Comand Party. LT. BOTHAM Q.C. promoted in 72 hours taan to BRUSSLS.	
Do	15-1-19		Receives letter. Re: CAPT. A.S. HOOPER R.A.M.C. (Late G.S. Brigade) with upto to their revit	
Do	16-1-19		to Duty on return from leave.	
Do			A/R.M.S. visits - (case repts) pursuing ie. (Ennche pneumonia). Deficience in hospitals.	
Do	17-1-19		Nothing to report.	
Do	18-1-19		Do. Brigad Brenard Freyemense — Cupt now b/ 11th R.Fe.	

Army Form C. 2118.
Page 160

WAR DIARY
of
INTELLIGENCE SUMMARY
(Erase heading not required.) 7a FIELD AMBCE

Instructions regarding War Diaries and Intelligence Summaries are contained in F. S. Regs., Part II. and the Staff Manual respectively. Title pages will be prepared in manuscript.

Place	Date	Hour	Summary of Events and Information	Remarks and references to Appendices
CROISON. Sheet 37 (In 33 Cadre)	19-1-19.		Listen in Cameron Front by military attack = Tournai.	[signature]
	20-1-19		Few walks. Reg. Jour at injur. Allotment of GC Readers for Demobilisation 20/1/19.	[init]
	21-1-19		Meeting of B.s of Cadres. Row. book takes at H.Q. 10 Obs.	[init]
	22-1-19		CAPT. R.A. HOPPER R.M.C 7. reports to duty this date. Nothing to report. First contention —	[init]
	23-1-19		CAPT. HOPPER R.M.C 7. to 6 E.S. for D.E. Interview with S.O.C. 10 Div : re Cadre's Advising Board & relieving to report. Reorganised Institutes.	[init]
	24-1-19			[init]
	25-1-19		Auste Cen. (Ron. Burdram ASPEK) slows in TOURNAI — whites & horn. rifpref. O.C. M.T. Corp. — Brew — gout.	[init]
	26-1-19		LT HOWLER informed by R.M.E. Row & fast convalid. Nothing to report.	[init]
	27-1-19		Cancelled betters at 2636 MONS — a Burial by Cylindrain at 27 RYMIN — Cancelled.	[init]
	28-1-19		Nothing to report.	[init]
	29-1-19		Road laid & tuspich thin. hopilised. Four and jans. Permit referred to 17 CCS. Both.	[init]
	30-1-19		Postmortem of towns good.	[init]
	31-1-19		Rainsed his mouth half a limit to BRJACK has been unaddudy (fort. Minus fustyless centre has been established in rall balm, and approx 6 b.l. hospal.	

[signature]
Major RAMC
OC 7a Fd. Ambce.

No. 7th Field Ambulance

Army Form C. 2118.

WAR DIARY
or
INTELLIGENCE SUMMARY.
(Erase heading not required.) 74th FIELD AMB. R.A.M.C. Page 161.

Instructions regarding War Diaries and Intelligence Summaries are contained in F. S. Regs., Part II. and the Staff Manual respectively. Title pages will be prepared in manuscript.

Place	Date	Hour	Summary of Events and Information	Remarks and references to Appendices
GRUGION (Nord) (27 cards) in M.I.S centres	1-2-19		Continuation of Evac and Fact "Activities" 3 places for Amb/lights proceeding weak.	
	2-2-19		Meeting of Estray Board - Pts. buildings in TURAN - against Chairman.	
do	3-2-19		Nothing to report. Fact continues.	
do	4-2-19		Card of hoping in lieu of buildings. Heil at HQ ambert Camp. - Wounders escorted 2 Line of can to Ser, Burner	
			S.S.M. Rafle NCC NCO reports to Orel.	
do	5-2-19		Hmes Boards Officer inspects and classifies all horses and units. Orders continues.	
do	6-2-19		Nothing to report. being to Railway Stn. ambulance cos for Officers in transity for Bosion etc. Err.	
do	7-2-19		Rail green Check to stm. road to Err. All continues as required.	
do	8-2-19		Nothing to report.	
do	9-2-19		Meeting of Board of Adm & Med. Fields - Army Ordinance Depot to inspect	
do	10-2-19		Nothing to report. Continued to report fact.	
do	11-2-19		Nothing to report.	
do	12-2-19			
do	13-2-19		Inspected "Returns" at Brigade Baths - found quite sufficient + reports accordingly.	
do	14-2-19		Nothing to report.	
do	15-2-19		Reopening Depot for Amb/lights.	
do	16-2-19		Cmdr proceeded to Tiflis write cards.	
do	17-2-19		Various Board reports. proceeded him t Bt. L. Torran. Reached here this eve. Short much march at GROZNY.	

16

War Diary / Intelligence Summary — Army Form C. 2118, Page 162

70th Field Ambulance

Place	Date	Hour	Summary of Events and Information	Remarks
GOUSON (N.33 Central) Chart 37	18-2-19		[illegible]	
	19-2-19			

140/35-37

17 JUL 1919

4th F.A.

Mar 1919

Army Form C 2118.

WAR DIARY
INTELLIGENCE SUMMARY.
(Erase heading not required.)

14th Field Ambulance. Page 163

Place	Date	Hour	Summary of Events and Information	Remarks and references to Appendices
GRISON Sheet 37 (N.33 Central)	1-3-19		Received Command of unit on return for leave to Paris.	
"	2-3-19		Eleven "Z" homes [illegible]	
"	3-3-19	3.15	Parade service. Nothing to report.	
"	4-3-19		Nothing to report.	
"	5-3-19	10 a.m.	Details of [illegible] of bombs & rockets — aircraft — & report rounds 29 R.H. m?	
"	"	a.m.	all to five 7 places line to service.	
"	6-3-19		Nothing to report — very unsettled weather — frequent rain.	
"	7-3-19	3.12	Nothing to report. 8 flares to investigate aloud this unit.	
"	8-3-19		Received Ypres Bailleul and Armentières — des malades.	
"	9-3-19		Nothing to report. Ordered to [illegible] train.	
"	10-3-19		Preparing to undertain. Nothing to report. M.Cpl Timothy Cumfield has a CYCLING.	
"	11-	3-19	Nothing to report. 2 Riders sent b/108 NFA — leaving of bread.	
"	12-3-19		Visited TOURNAI — Arranged to act as admin this return from Leave to Ca. McKenzie and returning [illegible]	
"	13-3-19		Go malade.	
"	14-3-19		Nothing to report.	
"	15-3-19		Nothing to report. Nursing of Bleury Road. Air buffetch in TOURNAI — refines along of booked service.	
"	16-3-19		Nothing to report.	

Army Form C. 2118.

WAR DIARY
or
INTELLIGENCE SUMMARY.
(Erase heading not required.)

74 FIELD AMBULANCE.

Page 164.

Instructions regarding War Diaries and Intelligence Summaries are contained in F. S. Regs., Part II. and the Staff Manual respectively. Title pages will be prepared in manuscript.

Place	Date	Hour	Summary of Events and Information	Remarks and references to Appendices
GRUSON Bett 27 (N.33 Central)	17-3-19		Warned that Rly. is being asked to cede traffic, and leaving TOURCOING before 21.3.19 – to concentrate at PRECIGVEANT. Was billeted estimating fr.	
	18-3-19		Last 4 horses cast away to HAVRE. only 5 mules remaining.	
	19-3-19		Handed over temporary charge unit to CAPT. P.W. ANDREW R.A.M.C. proceeding to England. leave 20/3/19	
	20.3	10	L.E. Lg. to St. Hyphal.	
	21.3	10		
	22.3	11	Lieut. IMBUSCH left with the O.C. awaiting instructions O.H.S.	
	23.3	19	happened to Brigadier permission for a report to proceeding to	
	24.3		London – G 1048 – 120	
			From Amiens Dept sent two R.H.S. personnel chargemen everyone once	
	25.3.19		Embus reported and returned to unit.	
	26.3.19		Only four cars running & a third. There is sure be little to do moving to Rouen – cancelled – and Calais is very arduous.	
			Expected to proceed.	
	27.3.19	4	Capt. P.W. & Moore received orders from 1st Corps. Proceed to Rouen etc. duty. Landed over temporary charge & went to C.O.	
	27.3.19		DENYER -> Died Ambulance (Referral Metz) from Capt. P.W. L. Andrews R.A.M.C. under resumed instruction from ADMS 34th Division.	
	28.3.19		No 90 Lt T.A GARRITT 19th Bn Durham Light Infy attached 74 Fd Amb Instr'n once on sick reported to Division for Centime. Surrendered 15/1/17 Ank. Ord 3rd Army to on sick.	
	29.3.19		Out reported. 3rd Army Ord. 27/3/19 to WHITE CYSOING ROM	
	30.3.19		Ret. remained from. RDM's 34 Div. 2 Corps. Under cover.	
	31.3.19		E'NCO. I. W. Of Re Priveles No. 114 to Corps Amzen'l Ret'n	

140/3000

26678

27 JUL 1919

Apr 1919

WAR DIARY
INTELLIGENCE SUMMARY

74th Field Ambulance — pages 165

Place	Date	Hour	Summary of Events and Information	Remarks and references to Appendices
Grierson M.33 Central 31.37 Belgian Army HQ France	1.4.19		Further instructions of MDMS 32nd Div. Nr. 53289 Re. O. Williamson RAMC presented for duty to No. 32 CCS. Interviewed & struck off strength on reaching UK.	AD
"	2.4.19		Nil report.	AD
"	3.4.19		Under two tractor DOST No. 71860/0/a A/31/3/19 Sunbeam Ambulance No. 17478 forwarded to DC 29 FAM Coy for return to Vehicle Depôt Rouen.	AD
"	4.4.19		M2/110527 Pte Ashby A.J. returned from leave to UK. 15/3/19 to 29/3/19. Lt. Col. E.C. Davidson returned from leave and assumed command of	AD Smith
"	5.4.19		Arrived 9/c of March strength (Fuel) Unit of 74 FA to Div.	Smith Nic.
"	6.4.19		Continuance of fine weather. Nothing to report.	P.P. Nic.
"	7.4.19		74th Field Ambulance arrived at Louvain and neighbourhood 6.45 pm. No 3 Ambulance of Division now concentrates in and "temp" billets in town & traps. Orders received to proceed to Revinde to England to report to OC Military H.D. Rochester Row, London to come on war Reserve. (DGMS 1087/157 Dated 3.4.19) Hands over command of Unit - informs O/C No 2 to Lt. Col. C.H. Denyer, M.C. Rome OC 72nd Field Ambulance.	Smith Nic.
"	8.4.19		Proceeded on leave Pte Clark, RAMC } Period 9/4/19 to 23/4/19 " Smith " Young	AD re same
"	9.4.19		Wilfrid Kraker Tank He M/304613 Pte Douglas G 4 Kraker Tank Coy 987 Coy RASC MT taken on strength WD. S.10.5-H D.D. & L. London, E.C. Bayne J. Forms/C2118/G.	

WAR DIARY / INTELLIGENCE SUMMARY

Army Form C. 2118.

Place	Date	Hour	Summary of Events and Information	Remarks and references to Appendices
Army Central M.33 Sh.37 Bit Ras-Malma	10.4.19		Nil report.	CRO
	11.4.19		Under instructions fr. RAMC Army Centre "A" No A96443 Sgt. Maj. T. Rug by RAMC proceeds this day to HQ 7. CLG (Agra-Fer-Arizona) near Aiwa for duty. Auth AQMS Front Area 1550/23 d/6.4.19	CRO
"	12.4.19		Nil report.	CRO
"	13.4.19		Nil report.	CRO
"	14.4.19		Nil report.	CRO
"	15.4.19		Communications from 73 Inf Bde. Arrangements being made for personnel to visit Bmmelo Anthony's Inquisita Ruins & Gua bagga. Name & Appendix to hand.	CRO
"	16.4.19		Therapy detailed for Temporary duty at 24 NH Bergh Church Township this day No. 1105116 Pte. Taylor RAMC " 104922 Pte Baltimo "	CRO
"	17.4.19		Nil report.	CRO
"	18.4.19		Nil report.	CRO
"	19.4.19		Nil report.	CRO
"	20.4.19		Easter Sunday. Holiday for all as many men to be spared as possible. Divine Service.	CRO
"	21.4.19		Easter Monday. Nil report.	CRO
"	22.4.19		102/3/2274 N° Munro Pte MT. for temp'y duty AQMS Office Tournai Proceeds on leave to U.K. per R. 24.4.19 to 8.5.19 George Pte Crunkhoh ? RAMC No 90978 Pte Powell 6. ? RAMC Brynd No 307096 (78247) " gives N.D. fr. Jelayso 6 O.R. for 3 days	CRO
"	23.4.19			CRO
"	24.4.19		1 N.O. 6.O.R. proceeded on short leave to Branch (This day). 50192 Staff Sgt. Bennett R.A.M.C. proceeded to U.K. on leave from 25.4.19 to 9.5.19 ORC.	CRO

Army Form C. 2118.

WAR DIARY
or
INTELLIGENCE SUMMARY.
(Erase heading not required.)

Instructions regarding War Diaries and Intelligence Summaries are contained in F. S. Regs., Part II. and the Staff Manual respectively. Title pages will be prepared in manuscript.

Place	Date	Hour	Summary of Events and Information	Remarks and references to Appendices
Gruson	25.4.19		144348 Pte P.W. WHITE R.A.M.C. Leave to U.K. 24.4.19 to 10-5-19.	W3@
m 33 Central	26.4.19		Nil report	W3@
Clar 3J	27.4.19		Nil report	W3@
Belg & Pay	28.4.19		Capt. W.B. Cathcart. m.o. R.A.M.C. took over command of this unit from Lt Col Denyer M.O. R.A.M.C.	W3@
France	29.4.19		Nil report	W3@
	30.4.19		Nil report	W3@

No. 74 Field Ambulance

WAR DIARY
INTELLIGENCE SUMMARY

Army Form C. 2118.

74th Field Amb.

Page 4

Place	Date	Hour	Summary of Events and Information	Remarks and references to Appendices
Cuillon	1.5.19	19	7H/111/240. Dvr. Daniels W.C. 12H/144/777 Dvr Davey C. RASC M.T. transferred for Zrs.Army H.T. Park, Valenciennes. 30.4.19. Struck off Strength. M2/131332 Pte Cinder, L/C R.A.S.C. M.T. evacuated — Burn (acc) 30.4.19.	W.D.2
M33 Centeal				
Sheet 37.	2.5.19	19	Nil Report.	W.D.2
Belgium	3.5.19	19	Surgeon Amb. Cpl. 14588 returned to Unit for duty. 7/11/17 to S.S.M. Rolfe. R.A.S.C. M.T. granted special leave to U.K. 4.5.19 - 18.5.19.	W.D.2
Part of France				
"	4.5.19	19	71/406 Sgt. Crawhurts. R.A.S.C. M.T. granted leave to U.K. 5.5.19 - 19.5.19.	W.D.2
"	5.5.19	19	Capt. W.F. Botkin. M.B. M.R.C. proceeded to "Replacements Depot." McArgrow for return to United States. Struck off Strength. 450008 Pte. Berner R.A.M.C. evacuated. 7605? Pte. Nichols. R.A.M.C. granted 40 days to U.K. 6.5.19. 20.5.19. 811164 Pte. Donald. G.H. R.A.M.C. granted leave to U.K. 7.5.19 - 21.5.19.	W.D.2
"	6.5.19	19		W.D.2
"	7.5.19	19	Nil Report.	W.D.2
"	8.5.19	19	5H/210459 Farr.Cpl. Jefford R.A.V.C. 49485 Pte. Oakley. R.A.M.C. 49452 Pte. Gontley. R.A.M.C. 53412 Pte. Nelson. E. to 5 Concentration Camp for demobilization.	W.D.2
"	9.5.19	19	102792 Pte. Hargreaved RAMC and 765282 Dvr. Baggley R.F.A. att: granted 6.mos. Furl. 9.5.19 - 23.5.19.	W.D.2
"	10.5.19	19	489041 Pte. Jones L/Cpl. R.A.M.C. Regmal. Unit for Genuine Reinforcement Base Depot. taken on Strength.	W.D.2
"	11.5.19	19	Nil Report.	W.D.2
"	12.5.19	19	36583 Sgt. Anning John 23131 Pte. Bowled. 49420 Pte. Clarke. 49054 Pte. Grant H.T. 65270 Pte. Strong. 79268 Pte. Nunly. 307086 Pte. Orr. 65288 Pte. Chuty. R.A.M.C. to 5 Concentration Camp for Dispersal. Struck off Strength.	W.D.2
"	13.5.19		Nil Report.	W.D.2
"	14.5.19		Nil Report.	W.D.2
"	15.5.19		Nil Report.	W.D.2

Army Form C. 2118.

WAR DIARY
or
INTELLIGENCE SUMMARY.

(Erase heading not required.)

Instructions regarding War Diaries and Intelligence Summaries are contained in F. S. Regs., Part II. and the Staff Manual respectively. Title pages will be prepared in manuscript.

Place	Date	Hour	Summary of Events and Information	Remarks and references to Appendices
Boulogne	16/5/19	19	Nil Report	10732
Stecle 37	17/5/19	19	Nil Report	10732
(M.93 Central)	18/5/19	19	No 4073 Pte Collier G.A. & No 9009 Pte Clifford A. R.A.M.C. to Con Camp for disposal. Struck off strength.	10732
	19/5/19	19	Nil Report	10732
	20/5/19	19	No.9057 Dvr Morton G.H. R.A.M.C. to 5th Concentration Camp for disposal. Struck off strength.	10732
	21/5/19	19	Nil Report	10732
	22/5/19	19	No. M/394613 Pte Daniel G. R.A.M.C. MT & Gunner Walsh J. and W.D 510524 returned to M. Notor Tank Coy.	10732
	23/5/19	19	Nil Report	10732
	24/5/19	19	1 W.O. & 6 O.Rs. R.A.M.C. proceeded to 5 Concentration Camp for disposal. 4 O.Rs proceeded on leave to U.K.	10732
	25/5/19	19	5 O.Rs. proceeded on leave to U.K. 27.5.19 to 10.6.19.	10732
	26/5/19	19	1 W.O. Returned, 30 R. R.A.M.C. proceeded on leave to U.K.	10732
	27/5/19	19	Nil Report	10732
	28/5/19	19	Nil Report	10732
	29/5/19	19	31447 Pte Morris G returned to duty date ab 51666d - No 29401 Pte Judd B returned from duty with 6th Sanitary Section	10732
	30/5/19	19	4 O.Rs transferred (strength off strength) to 7 T.C.B.S. for duty	10732
	31/5/19	19	Nil Report	10732

www.ingramcontent.com/pod-product-compliance
Lightning Source LLC
Chambersburg PA
CBHW080907230426
43664CB00016B/2751